A WOMAN'S WORLD
IN CROSS STITCH

Over **40** designs to make you smile

Joan Elliott

D&C
David and Charles

For my grandmothers
Elizabeth Urban and Theresa Elliott

A DAVID & CHARLES BOOK
Copyright © David & Charles Limited 2008

David & Charles is an F+W Publications Inc. company
4700 East Galbraith Road
Cincinnati, OH 45236

First published in the UK in 2008

A catalogue record for this book is available from the British Library.

ISBN-13: 978-0-7153-2673-2 hardback
ISBN-10: 0-7153-2673-2 hardback

ISBN-13: 978-0-7153-2674-9 paperback
ISBN-10: 0-7153-2674-0 paperback

Printed in China by Shenzen RR Donnelly Printing Co.Ltd.
for David & Charles
Brunel House   Newton Abbot   Devon

Executive Editor Cheryl Brown
Desk Editor Bethany Dymond
Project Editor and Chart Preparation Lin Clements
Senior Designer Charly Bailey
Photography Kim Sayer and Karl Adamson
Production Controller Ros Napper

Visit our website at www.davidandcharles.co.uk

David & Charles books are available from all good bookshops; alternatively
you can contact our Orderline on 0870 9908222 or write to us at FREEPOST
EX2 110, D&C Direct, Newton Abbot, TQ12 4ZZ (no stamp required UK only);
US customers call 800-289-0963 and Canadian customers call 800-840-5220.

Contents

Introduction...4

Material Girls 6

Woodland Goddess..................16

Teatime Tittle-Tattle...............24

Working Women 32

Domestic Angels 40

The Art of Aging Gracefully...................56

Victorian Lady's Garden.........................66

Sweet Indulgence....................74

For All the Women I Am 82

Sea Goddess 92

Useful Information 100

About the Author 104

Suppliers......................................104

Acknowledgments..............................105

Index.......................................105

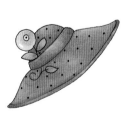

Introduction

There have always been special qualities that women in particular seem to embrace: love, compassion, capability and endurance are all words that easily come to mind. The generations that have come before us pass on the knowledge gained through their life experiences. I've dedicated this book to my grandmothers who were both strong, courageous women. Grandma Elizabeth fled Poland in the early 1900s with five young children in tow. Nana Theresa, American born and widowed at an early age, found herself raising two young boys through the Depression. Through the years I could see where my own parents learned their strength and loving nature and I feel blessed that this very quality passes through each generation that follows. I know that many of us share similar stories. We all reap the benefits of women's history – be it the campaign for women's suffrage, women entering the work force, or the women's liberation movement – and so comes the inspiration for this book, focused entirely on our world.

Whimsy, fantasy and expressions of love are worked into a collection of designs that celebrate some of the many aspects of what it means to be a female. You'll find a chapter that recognizes the material girl in all of us, filled with accessories to help you 'shop 'til you drop', and for all hardworking domestic angels there are projects to celebrate the cook, the stitcher and the woman that just has to do-it-herself.

Using sparkling metallic threads, beads and hand-dyed fabrics, two beautiful goddesses take you deep into the sea and woods on a journey of pure fantasy. Walk through a Victorian lady's garden and learn how flowers symbolize the finer characteristics inherent in all women.

Make merry with the girls, share confidences and discuss the latest tittle-tattle over a mug of coffee or cup of tea. Should you indulge in chocolate cake while you are chatting, there's a bevy of bovines to help ease you through your sweet indulgence. A whimsical tribute to working women lightens the burden of daily routines. Speaking of things that may weigh heavily on us, there's a chapter encouraging us to make sure that no matter how we age or how quickly the years go by, we will age gracefully. For all the women we are, there are lovely keepsake projects for sisters, mothers, grandmothers and daughters.

I do hope that within the chapters that follow you will find something to make you smile, spark your imagination, inspire pride and help you celebrate all the joys of womanhood.

Material Girls

So much to shop for . . . so little time. What's a girl to do? Let go and indulge your every material need with these three pictures and matching accessories to make your shopping spree go smoothly.

The picture on page 9 should give you some inspiration – will you step out in your best cowgirl boots, elegant slides or gold-embroidered stilettos? After all, owning fab shoes doesn't have much to do with actually *needing* them but oh, the pleasure of wearing them!

Lunch with the girls is the perfect occasion for the right hat. A sassy beret, diamond-studded cowgirl hat, a retro mod tam or your duly deserved tiara ... which will you choose?

I'm sure that we can all agree that the most essential accessory of all is the perfect bag. Be it a gaily coloured tote, a leopard skin clutch, or an embroidered Victorian purse, it seems that there are never enough bags in our wardrobe. Stitch up a co-ordinated chequebook (checkbook) cover, notebook and key ring and you'll be more than ready to 'shop 'til you drop'!

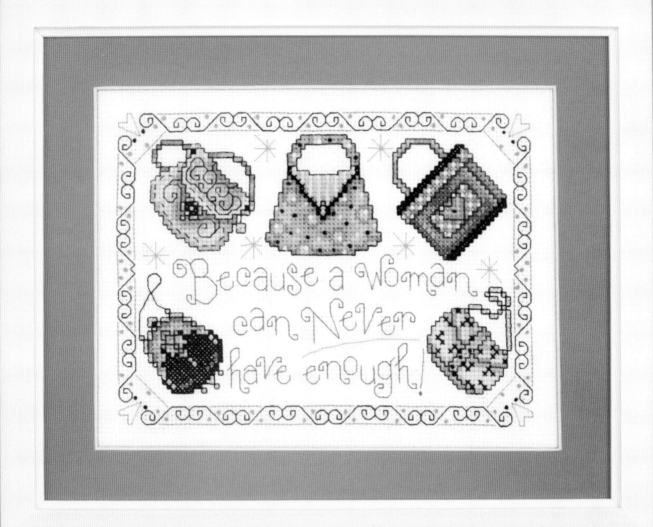

Because a Woman can Never have enough!

Let's Shop Pictures

Bags, hats, shoes… the hard part is knowing which to choose! Stitch up one of these notices for that special friend you must have along when you go shopping.

Stitch count (each design)
70h x 98w
Design size (each design)
12.7 x 18cm (5 x 7in)

Go Shop! (for each picture)
✦ 25.5 x 30.5cm (10 x 12in) white 14-count Aida
✦ Tapestry needle size 24 and a beading needle
✦ DMC stranded cotton (floss) as listed in chart key
✦ Kreinik #4 Very Fine Braid 028 citron
✦ Mill Hill Magnifica™ glass beads 10028 silver

1 Prepare for work, referring to page 100 if necessary. Find and mark the centre of the fabric and the centre of the relevant chart on pages 12–14. Mount your fabric in an embroidery frame if you wish.

2 Start stitching from the centre of the chart, using two strands of stranded cotton (floss) for cross stitches. Use one strand to stitch all Kreinik #4 braid cross stitches and backstitches. Work all other backstitches with one strand. Following the chart for colour changes, work all French knots using one strand wrapped twice around the needle. Using a beading needle and matching thread, attach the beads (see page 101) according to the positions shown on the chart.

3 Once all the stitching is complete, finish your picture by mounting and framing (see page 102).

A WOMAN'S WIT. . .
When the going gets tough. . .
the tough go shopping!

Stiletto Key Ring

Stitch count 21h x 27w
Design size 3 x 3.8cm (1⅛ x 1½in)

Decorated with a gold-embroidered high-heeled shoe, there will be no more hunting for keys at the bottom of your bag once you attach them to this key ring. Stitch the design on a 10.2cm (4in) square of white 18-count Aida following the chart and key on page 15. Use two strands of stranded cotton for cross stitches and one strand of Kreinik thread. Work backstitches with one strand. Work French knots with one strand wrapped twice around the needle.

Back the finished embroidery with iron-on interfacing following the manufacturer's instructions and trim to fit a 5.7cm (2¼in) diameter acrylic key ring. Cut a circle of coloured card the same size, place behind the stitching and assemble in the key ring.

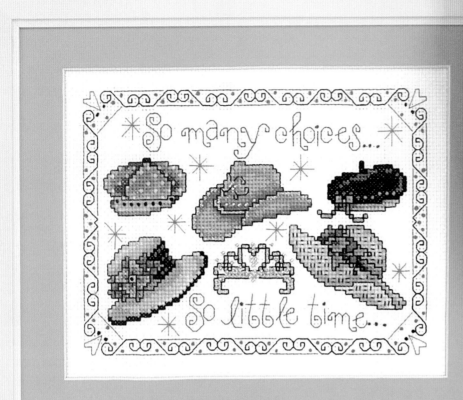

So many choices...

So little time...

What does need have to do with it?

Chequebook Cover

If writing cheques is getting to be a humdrum chore, add some pizzazz to your spending and some fun to your funds with this cheeky chequebook cover.

Stitch count
34h x 76w

Design size
6.2 x 13.8cm (2½ x 5½in)

Go Shop!
+ 25.4 x 28cm (10 x 11in) white 14-count Aida
+ Tapestry needle size 24 and a beading needle
+ Kreinik #4 Very Fine Braid 028 citron
+ DMC stranded cotton (floss) as listed in chart key
+ Mill Hill Magnifica™ glass beads 10028 silver
+ Clear vinyl chequebook cover (available at most craft and needlework shops)
+ Two pieces of lightweight white card to fit finished stitching

1 Prepare for work, referring to page 100 if necessary. Fold the Aida in half and mark the centre of the bottom half of the fabric. This will leave the top half blank for the back of the chequebook cover. Find the centre of the chart on page 15. Mount your fabric in an embroidery frame if you wish.

2 Start stitching from the centre of the chart, using two strands of stranded cotton (floss) for cross stitches. Use one strand to stitch all Kreinik #4 braid cross stitches and backstitches. Work all other backstitches with one strand. Following the chart for colour changes, work all French knots using one strand wrapped twice around the needle. Using a beading needle and matching thread, attach the beads (see page 101) according to the positions shown on the chart.

3 Once all the stitching is complete, place the opened chequebook cover over your finished embroidery and trim the embroidery to fit. Slip your embroidery inside the cover. Cut two pieces of white card to fit behind the embroidery and slip into place. Your chequebook is now ready for some serious shopping!

Tiara Notebook

If you have oodles of things to buy and want to keep track of it all, this little bejewelled notebook will slip easily into your purse and is fit for the most deserving princess.

Stitch count
67h x 43w

Design size
12.2 x 7.8cm (4¾ x 3in)

Go Shop!
- 25.4 x 20.3cm (10 x 8in) white 14-count Aida
- Tapestry needle size 24 and a beading needle
- Kreinik #4 Very Fine Braid 028 citron
- DMC stranded cotton (floss) as listed in chart key
- Mill Hill Magnifica™ glass beads 10028 silver
- Lightweight iron-on interfacing
- 50.8cm (20in) decorative trim to tone with embroidery
- One decorative satin rose
- 19 x 12cm (7½ x 4¾in) notebook (available at stationers)
- Permanent fabric glue

1 Prepare for work, referring to page 100 if necessary. Find and mark the centre of the fabric and centre of the chart on page 15. Stitch the design as step 2 opposite.

2 Make up the journal as follows. Cut iron-on interfacing 2.5cm (1in) larger than the finished embroidery all round. With the embroidery wrong side up on some thick towels, centre the interfacing on it and use a medium iron to fuse it to the embroidery. Trim the embroidery four rows beyond the design. Centre the embroidery on the journal cover and attach using permanent fabric glue. Glue decorative trim along the raw edge of the embroidery, starting and ending at centre bottom, attaching a satin rose where the ends meet.

A WOMAN'S WIT. . .
I have always felt that a gift diamond shines so much brighter than one you buy for yourself.
(Mae West)

DMC stranded cotton
Cross stitch

	208
/	209
	210
●	310
	312
	317
—	318
T	334
	415
V	602
	603
	604
	676
L	677
/	729
	743
Y	744
H	905
	906
	907
	3755
	3829
·	blanc
	Kreinik #4 braid 028 citron (1 strand)

Backstitch
—— 310
—— 312
—— 602

French knots
● 310
● 312
● 602

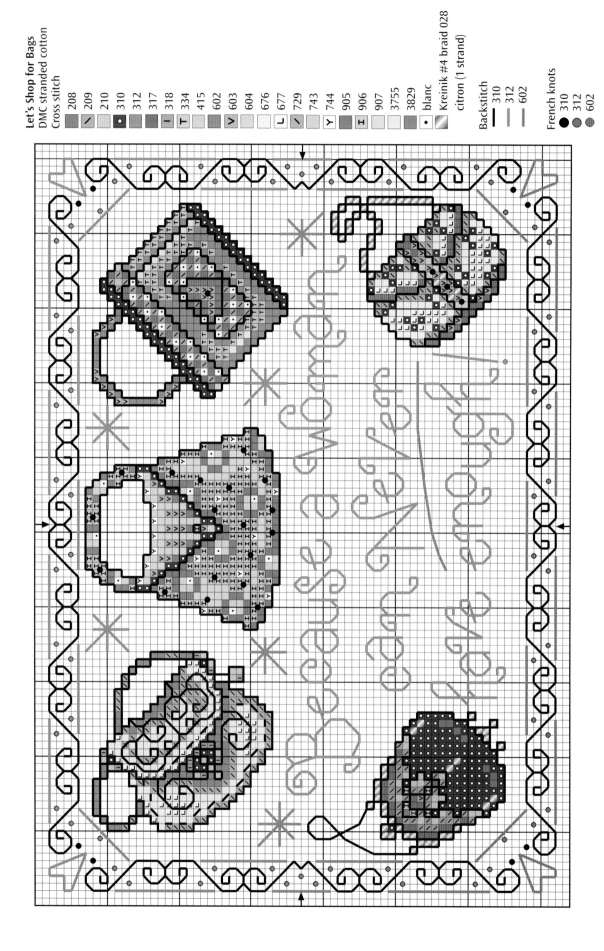

Let's Shop for Hats
DMC stranded cotton
Cross stitch

208	209	210	310	312	317	334	601	602	603	604	676	677	729	742	743	744	905	906	907	3755	Kreinik #4 braid

028 citron (1 strand)

Backstitch
310
312
602

French knots
310
312
602

Mill Hill seed beads
10028 silver

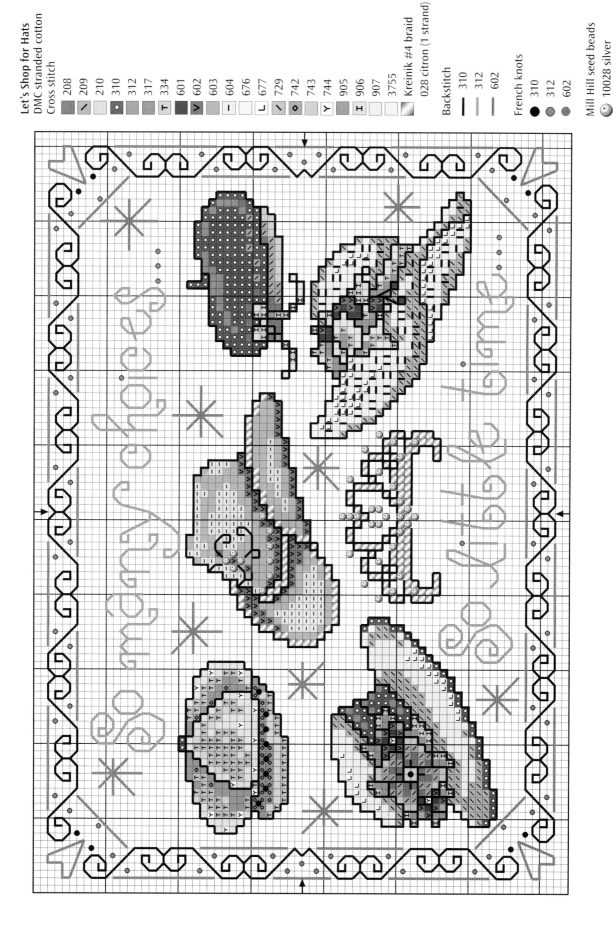

13

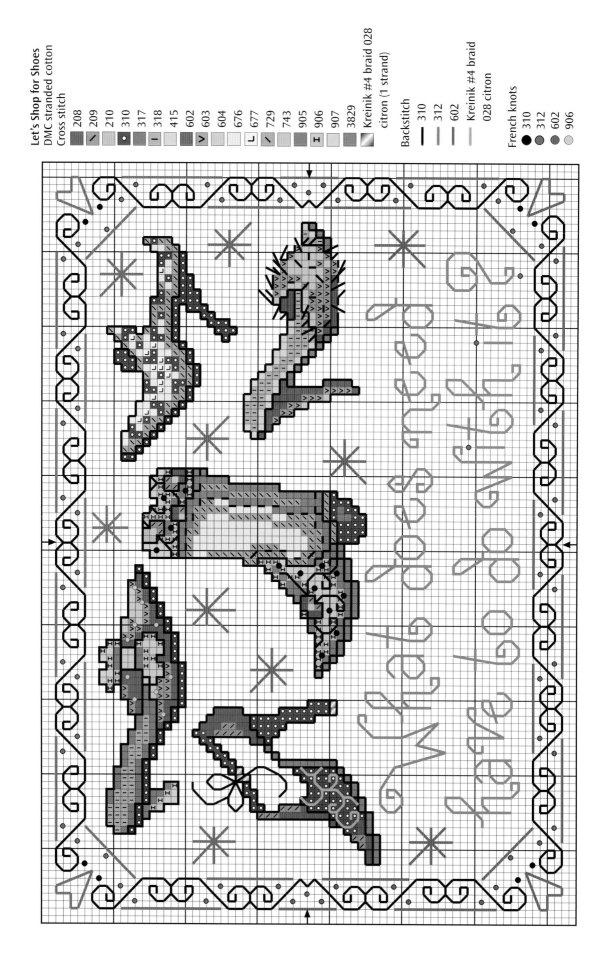

Let's Shop for Shoes

DMC stranded cotton

Cross stitch

208	
209	
210	
310	
317	
318	
415	
602	
603	
604	
676	
677	
729	
743	
905	
906	
907	
3829	
Kreinik #4 braid 028 citron (1 strand)	

Backstitch

— 310
— 312
— 602
Kreinik #4 braid
028 citron

French knots

● 310
● 312
● 602
○ 906

Chequebook Cover

Key Ring

Notebook

Material Girls' Accessories
DMC stranded cotton

Cross stitch		Backstitch	
208		▬▬	310
209		▬▬	312
310		▬▬	602
312		▬▬	Kreinik #4 braid
334	T		028 citron
602			
905		**French knots**	
906	I	●	310
Kreinik #4 braid		●	312
028 citron		●	602
(1 strand)			

Mill Hill seed beads
10028 silver

Woodland Goddess

*I*magine an early morning walk through the deepest part of the forest. Life is hidden everywhere – beneath the leafy forest floor, around each majestic tree, under every moss-covered stone. In a small clearing ahead you hear a rustling of leaves, glimpse a flicker of magical light and as you draw closer you see her, the woodland goddess tiptoeing softly through her silent realm. Falling leaves, glistening vines and flowers of sweet woodruff adorn her gown. Her lustrous wings sparkle in the filtered light and beads of morning dew float all around her. In her hand a tiny bird has come to rest. At her feet, wild creatures gather round, mushrooms sprout and a nest filled with tiny eggs holds the promise of new life.

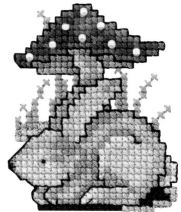

Choose a delicious hand-dyed evenweave to stitch this beautiful design on or use one of the many solid colours of evenweave or Aida that you will find in your local needlework shop. Two additional designs have been used to create a pretty little sachet and a charming little greetings card.

16

Woodland Goddess Picture

Step into the mythical realm of the Woodland Goddess and visit with the friends of the forest that surround her. If you listen closely you might here the soft flutter of her gossamer wings.

Stitch count
245h x 189w

Design size
44.5 x 34.3cm (17½ x 13½in)

Go Shop!
✦ 58.5 x 48.3cm (23 x 19in) fallen leaves 28-count hand-dyed Jobelan (Polstitches – see Suppliers)
✦ Tapestry needle size 24 and a beading needle
✦ DMC stranded cotton (floss) as listed in chart key
✦ Kreinik #4 Very Fine Braid (2 spools of each) as listed in chart key
✦ Kreinik blending filament 032 pearl
✦ Mill Hill glass seed beads as listed in chart key

1 Prepare for work, referring to page 100 if necessary. Mark the centre of the fabric and centre of the chart on pages 20–23. For your own use you could photocopy the chart parts and tape them together. Mount your fabric in an embroidery frame if you wish.

2 Start stitching from the centre of the chart and fabric, working over two fabric threads and using two strands of stranded cotton (floss) for full and three-quarter cross stitches. Working in one direction and using one strand of blending filament, overstitch the DMC 164 and 369 cross stitches in the wings. Work French knots using one strand wound twice around the needle. Use one strand to stitch Kreinik #4 braid cross stitches and backstitches. Work all other backstitches and long stitches with one strand. Using a beading needle and matching thread, attach the beads (see page 101) as shown on the chart.

3 Once stitching is complete, mount and frame your picture (see page 102).

18

Moth Sachet and Mushroom Card

Stitch count (each design) 30h x 30w
Design size (each design) 5.4 x 5.4cm (2⅛ x 2⅛in)

A woodland luna moth adorns a sachet creating a precious treasure to fill with fragrant pot-pourri, while a bird's nest and pearl-embellished mushroom make a delightful card. Both motifs are interchangeable and make sweet tokens of affection. For each design you will need: 17.8cm (7in) square of blue 28-count Lugana (Zweigart code 513); threads and Mill Hill beads as listed in the chart key. For the sachet you will need 17.8cm (7in) of decorative cord for hanging and a small tassel. For the card use a ready-made aperture card.

Follow the charts here, using two strands of stranded cotton (floss) for full and three-quarter cross stitches and one strand for backstitches. Use one strand for Kreinik #4 Very Fine Braid cross stitches. Work French knots using one strand wound twice around the needle. Attach beads with a beading needle and matching thread. Once stitching is complete, mount the embroidery into a card (see page 101) or make up into a mini sachet (see page 103). See page 103 for making a twisted cord and a tassel.

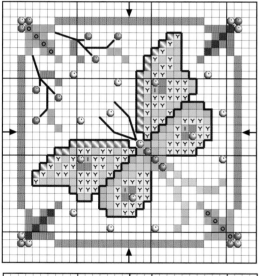

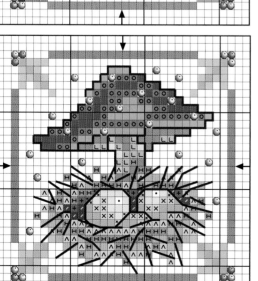

Moth and Mushroom
DMC stranded cotton
Cross stitch

	315		3024
+	434	H	3045
	471		3046
	597	∧	3047
×	598		3347
╱	801	Y	3348
	831		3811
I	832	O	3826
	975		3857
	976	•	blanc
	3022		Kreinik #4 braid 105V vintage amber (1 strand)
L	3023		

Backstitch
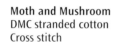 938

Mill Hill seed beads
- 00374 rainbow
- 02038 brilliant copper
- 03021 royal pearl

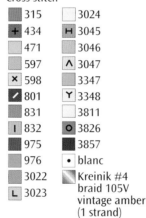

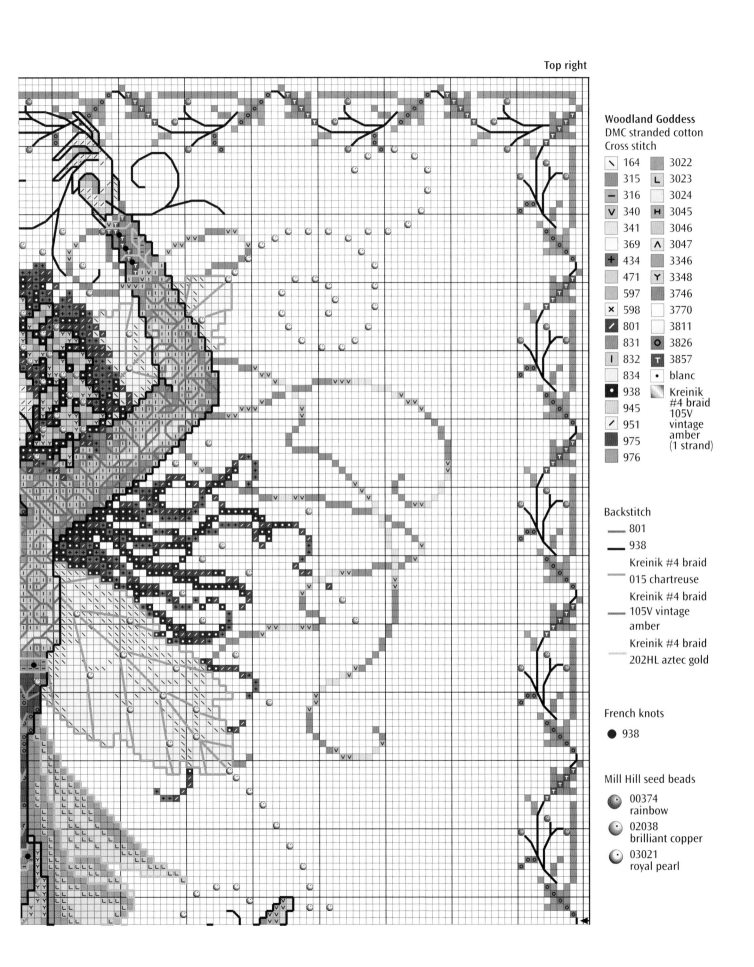

Woodland Goddess
DMC stranded cotton
Cross stitch

＼	164		3022
	315	L	3023
─	316		3024
V	340	H	3045
	341		3046
	369	∧	3047
＋	434		3346
	471	Y	3348
	597		3746
×	598		3770
／	801		3811
	831	O	3826
I	832	T	3857
	834	•	blanc
◉	938		Kreinik #4 braid 105V vintage amber (1 strand)
	945		
╱	951		
	975		
	976		

Backstitch

— 801

— 938

Kreinik #4 braid
015 chartreuse

Kreinik #4 braid
105V vintage
amber

Kreinik #4 braid
202HL aztec gold

French knots

● 938

Mill Hill seed beads

◉ 00374
rainbow

◉ 02038
brilliant copper

◉ 03021
royal pearl

21

Bottom left

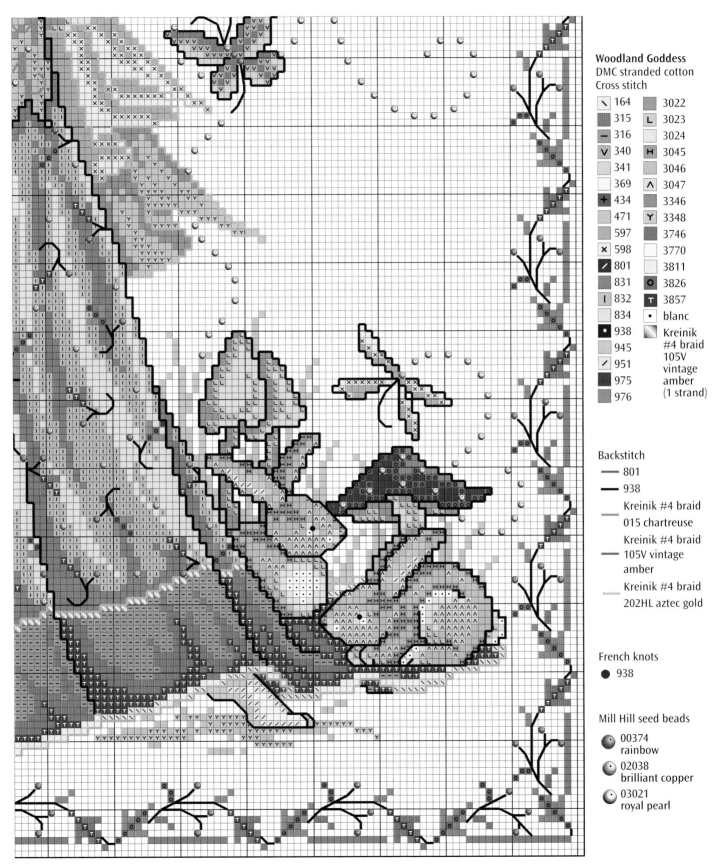

Woodland Goddess
DMC stranded cotton
Cross stitch

⟍	164		3022
	315	L	3023
−	316		3024
V	340	H	3045
	341		3046
	369	∧	3047
+	434		3346
	471	Y	3348
	597		3746
×	598		3770
╱	801		3811
	831	⊙	3826
I	832	T	3857
	834	•	blanc
◉	938		Kreinik
	945		#4 braid
╱	951		105V
	975		vintage
	976		amber
			(1 strand)

Backstitch
— 801
— 938
— Kreinik #4 braid
   015 chartreuse
— Kreinik #4 braid
   105V vintage
   amber
··· Kreinik #4 braid
   202HL aztec gold

French knots
● 938

Mill Hill seed beads
◉ 00374
   rainbow
◉ 02038
   brilliant copper
◉ 03021
   royal pearl

Bottom right

Teatime Tittle-Tattle

A fresh cup of richly brewed coffee or a soothing cup of your favourite tea – no matter which you prefer both are the perfect elixirs to sip together with the girls. Whether we are indulging in teatime tittle-tattle or coffee-pot confidences, over steaming cups we can share small talk, catch up on the latest news and confide our deepest feelings. We meet to soothe our souls and to share a well-deserved giggle.

In this design, collectible teapots of delicately decorated porcelain sit nicely within a lacy border, reminding us that in the end, friends are always the best collectibles. Overleaf a colourful array of coffee mugs and a basket of fresh-baked biscuits celebrate good friends and a good life.

Two matching coasters with an extra wink of humour make the perfect place to rest your cups while you chat. The designs are so quick to stitch that making up a set for the group would be fun and easy to do.

Beverage Friends Pictures

Whether you switch on the kettle for tea or brew some rich roasted coffee, there is nothing quite like getting together with your friends for some good conversation over a cup of one of these magical elixirs.

Stitch count (each picture)
97h x 125w
Design size (each picture)
17.8 x 23cm (7 x 9in)

Go Shop!
✦30.5 x 35.5cm (12 x 14in)
  14-count antique white
  Aida (Tea design)
✦30.5 x 35.5cm (12 x 14in)
  14-count Fiddler's Light
  Aida (Coffee design)
✦Tapestry needle size 24
✦DMC stranded cotton (floss)
  as listed in chart key

1 Prepare for work, referring to page 100 if necessary. Mark the centre of the fabric and centre of the chart on pages 28–29 (or pages 30–31). Mount fabric in an embroidery frame if you wish.

2 Start stitching from the centre of the chart and fabric. Use two strands of stranded cotton (floss) for full and three-quarter cross stitches. Work French knots using two strands wound once around the needle. Use one strand for backstitches.

3 Once all the stitching is complete, finish your picture by mounting and framing (see page 102).

A WOMAN'S WIT. . .
*It takes a long time to
grow an old friend.*

Gossip Coasters

Stitch count (each coaster) 40h x 39w
Design size 7 x 7cm (2¾ x 2¾in)

While sharing a bit of harmless gossip you can set your tea cup or coffee mug down on these fun coasters. For one coaster you will need: 20.3cm (8in) square of antique white 14-count Aida (or Fiddler's Light Aida) and a Lucite coaster (see Suppliers). Following the chart on page 29 or 31, work cross stitches with two strands of stranded cotton (floss) and backstitches with one strand. Work French knots using two strands wrapped once around the needle. Mount your embroidery in the coaster according to the manufacturer's instructions.

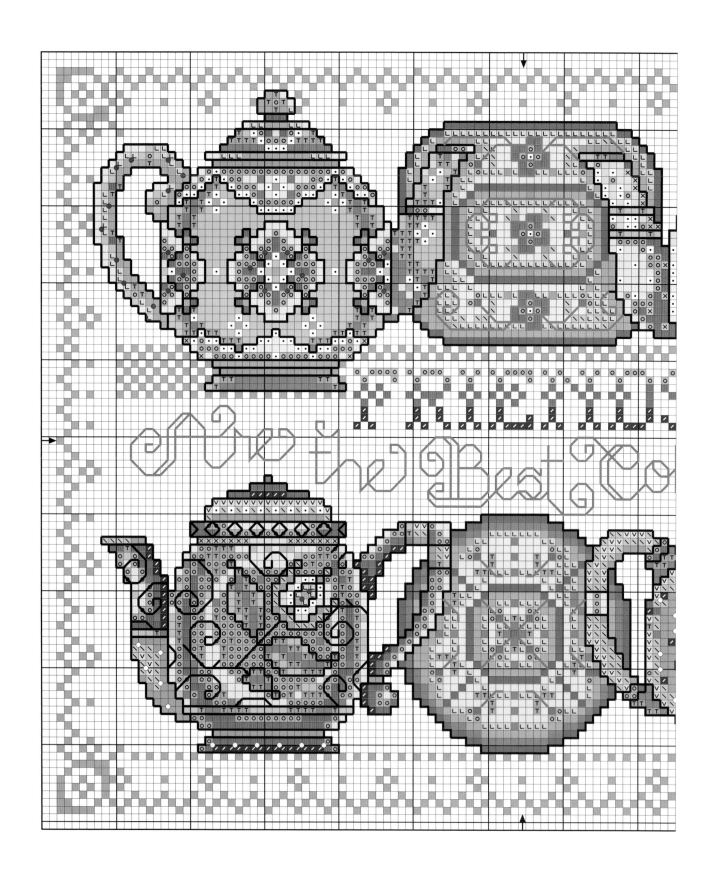

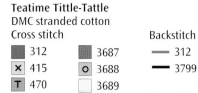

Teatime Tittle-Tattle
DMC stranded cotton
Cross stitch

■	312	▨	3687	
✕	415	○	3688	
T	470	▦	3689	
▨	471	▨	3803	
▨	502	V	3813	
╲	503	L	3821	
▦	762	▦	3822	
▨	932	▨	3852	
■	3346	•	blanc	

Backstitch
— 312
— 3799

French knots
● 312
● 3799
○ blanc

Teatime Coaster
DMC stranded cotton
Cross stitch

■	3346	▦	3689
▨	3687	▨	3803
○	3688		

Backstitch
— 312
— 3799

French knots
● 312

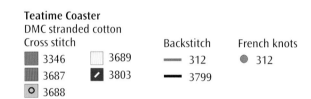

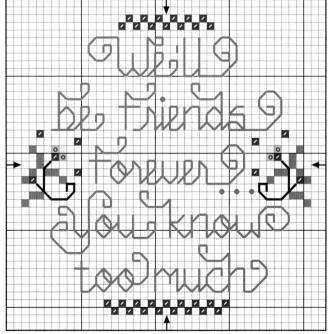

29

Coffee-Pot Confidences
DMC stranded cotton
Cross stitch

■ 312		⊡ 898		
L 334		V 906		
○ 350		907		
351		N 3325		
415		⁄ 3371		
434		\ 3753		
∧ 436		3755		
437		T 3820		
⁄ 676		3822		
701		+ 3829		
✕ 729		3852		
762		• blanc		
■ 817				

Backstitch
— 312
— 898
— 3371

French knots
● 312
● 898
● 3371

Coffee-Time Coaster
DMC stranded cotton
Cross stitch

312	■ 817	
L 334	T 3820	
○ 350	3852	
701		

Backstitch
— 312
— 3371

French knots
● 312
● 3371

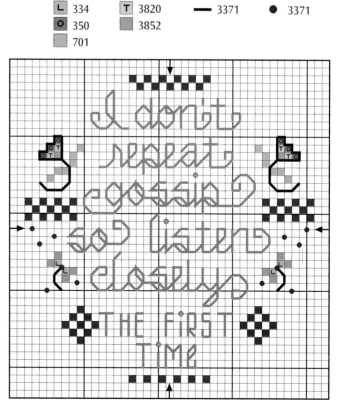

Working Women

Which one of the two women shown opposite are you – the frazzled go-getter who tries to do it all or the laid-back creature who doesn't let work interfere with looking beautiful? There's no doubt that at times the working world can seem like a never-ending treadmill with no way to jump off. So ladies, let's keep our sense of humour through it all and show the world a little attitude!

Is your 'in-tray' piled high with things to do, is your mobile phone forever trilling and the clock ticking way too fast? Do you feel scattered about in so many places it barely seems worth it to get dressed properly or put on any make-up? Are you so overwhelmed with queries that you can't possibly have an answer for them all? If so, these four witty designs are sure to lighten up your work place. The designs can also adorn other items, such as a tote bag, shown on page 35.

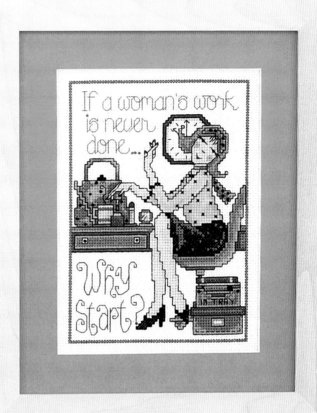

Some Work Days. . .

A WOMAN'S WIT. . .
I am woman, I am invincible, I am tired!

Oh my! Don't we all have days that seem like they will never end, filled with memos and errands and stress? Rise up with a smile on your face and just show them who's boss!

Stitch count (each design)
97h x 69w

Design size (each design)
17.7cm x 12.5cm (7 x 5in)

Go Shop!
- 30.5 x 25.4cm (12 x 10in) 14-count white Aida
- Tapestry needle size 24
- DMC stranded cotton (floss) as listed in chart key

1 Prepare for work, referring to page 100 if necessary. Mark the centre of the fabric and chart (pages 36–39). Use an embroidery frame if you wish. Note that the Don't Ask Me design is landscape shaped (wider), not portrait-shaped as the other three designs.

2 Start stitching from the centre of the chart and fabric. Use two strands of stranded cotton (floss) for full and three-quarter cross stitches. Work French knots using two strands wound once around the needle. Following the chart colours, use one strand for backstitches. If you wish to change the hair and skin colours, use the key overleaf.

3 Once stitching is complete, mount and frame your picture (see page 102) or make up as a tote bag as described on page 102. You could also use the design as a patch to apply to a variety of ready-made items, such as notebooks or boxes.

A WOMAN'S WIT. . .
Being organized interferes with my creativity.

Some Days . . .
DMC stranded cotton
Cross stitch

⊙	310
/	318
↓	350
	415
	434
	552
V	553
	602
O	603
	604
\	676
	729
	742
×	743
	744
	798
	799
	801
\	817
	905
T	906
	907
I	945
	951
L	3829
•	blanc

Backstitch

——	310
——	552
——	799
——	817

French knots

● 310

To change skin and
hair colours, use
the chart below and
opposite

Changing Skin Tone and Hair Colour

Use the DMC stranded cotton shades here to change the skin tones
to those of your choice. For example, to change a White skin tone
to Black, use 435 instead of 951. Cheek colour would remain
unchanged. This chart also allows you to choose a light, medium
or dark look. Hair colour can be changed in a similar way by
substituting the colours given in the charts for those listed here.

Skin Colour	White	Black	Hispanic	Asian
Light	951	435	437	3770
Medium	945	434	436	951
Dark	3771	433	435	945

Work is Never Done. . .
DMC stranded cotton
Cross stitch

◎	310
▨	317
╱	318
▾	350
▨	415
▨	553
▨	602
○	603
▨	604
^	729
▨	742
×	743
	744
▨	798
◥	817
▨	869
▨	905
T	906
▨	907
I	945
	951
▨	3829
•	blanc

Backstitch

——	310
——	796
——	817

French knots

●	310
●	796
●	817

To change skin and hair colours, use the the chart opposite and below

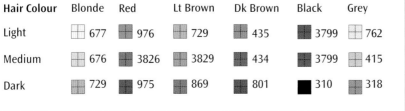

Hair Colour	Blonde	Red	Lt Brown	Dk Brown	Black	Grey
Light	▦ 677	▨ 976	▨ 729	▨ 435	▨ 3799	▦ 762
Medium	▦ 676	▨ 3826	▨ 3829	▨ 434	▨ 3799	▦ 415
Dark	▨ 729	▨ 975	▨ 869	▨ 801	■ 310	▨ 318

Born to Shop
DMC stranded cotton
Cross stitch

⊙	310
	552
V	553
	554
	602
O	604
	742
	743
	798
L	799
	809
\	817
	869
	906
	907
I	945
	951
\	3829

Backstitch
—— 310
—— 817

To change skin and
hair colours, use the
chart on page 36

A WOMAN'S WIT. . .
*I'm usually gorgeous,
but this is my day off.*

Don't Ask Me

DMC stranded cotton
Cross stitch

◉	310
╱	434
	552
V	553
	602
O	603
	604
	742
X	743
	744
	798
L	799
	801
	809
╱	817
	906
	907
I	945
•	951
•	blanc

Backstitch
—— 310
—— 817

French knots
● 310

To change skin and
hair colours, use the
chart on page 36

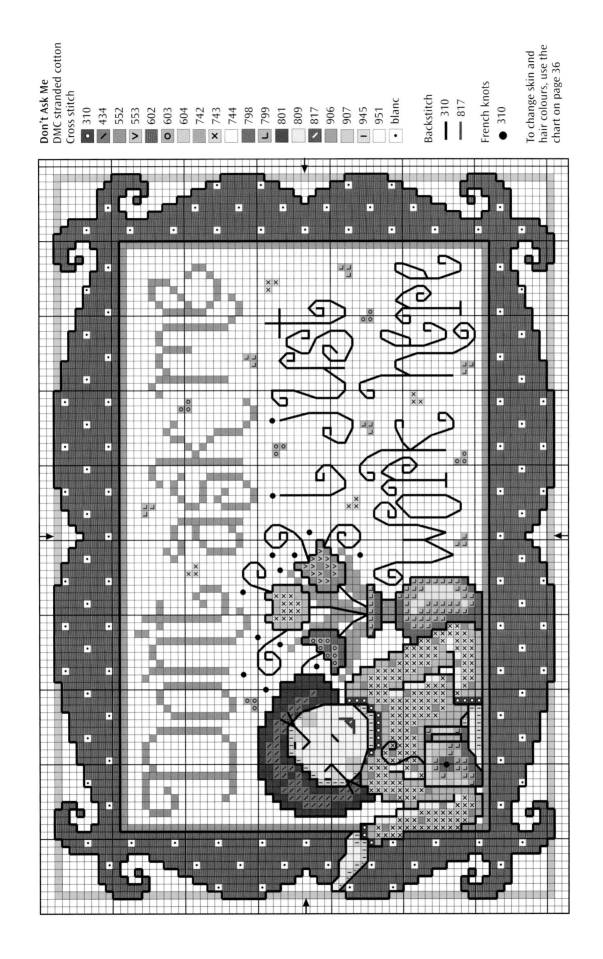

Domestic Angels

A versatile woman can find joy in her everyday tasks and allow her angelic side to always shine through. Love to stitch, cook, or putter around the house? If so, here are three angels that are happy to join you in your pursuits. A box of recipes, fresh-from-the-oven apple pie, pots, pans and utensils in hand, our capable cooking angel opposite has today's menu completely under control. Made up into a cheerful three-ring binder she will help you keep all your favourite recipes neatly organized and close at hand.

To keep you company while you 'measure twice and cut once' a handy do-it-yourself angel on page 45 is complete with her well-stocked tool box, paint, pliers and the essential roll of duct tape. Surrounded by all the bits, buttons and bobs that can be found in a stitcher's closet, a sweet stitching angel on page 47 reminds everyone that cross stitchers are X-tra special people.

Cooking Angel Recipe Book

Keep all your cooking secrets close at hand and protected inside this cheerful covered binder and in no time at all you can whip up a miraculous recipe to wow your family or special guests.

Stitch count
131h x 103w

Design size
24 x 19cm (9½ x 7½in)

Go Shop!
- 37 x 32cm (14½ x 12½in) antique white 14-count Aida
- Tapestry needle size 24 and a beading needle
- DMC stranded cotton (floss) as listed in chart key
- Kreinik #4 Very Fine Braid 150V vintage amber
- Mill Hill™ glass seed beads 02038 brilliant copper
- Lightweight iron-on interfacing
- One three-ring binder 29 x 27cm (11½ x 10½in)
- 0.5m (½yd) white cotton batting or felt
- 0.5m (½yd) fabric for outside cover to tone with embroidery
- 0.5m (½yd) fabric for inside covers to tone
- 0.5m (½yd) narrow ribbon to tone with embroidery
- Two pieces 27 x 24cm (10½ x 9½in) heavy white card
- 1.4m (1½yd) decorative trim to tone with embroidery
- Spray craft adhesive and permanent fabric glue
- One decorative button

1 Prepare for work, referring to page 100 if necessary. Mark the centre of the fabric and chart on pages 50–51.

2 Start stitching from the centre of the chart, using two strands of stranded cotton for cross stitches. Use one strand for all Kreinik stitches. Use two strands of white to backstitch 'Bon Apetit'. Work all other backstitches with one strand. Work French knots using one strand wrapped twice around the needle. Using a beading needle and matching thread, attach the beads (see page 101) as charted.

3 Once stitching is complete, make up the book cover as follows. Cut iron-on interfacing 2.5cm (1in) larger than the finished embroidery all around. With the wrong side facing, centre the interfacing and fuse to the embroidery. Trim the embroidery eight rows beyond the design.

4 Open the binder and lay it flat on the batting or felt. Trace the outline of the binder on to the batting or felt and cut. In a well-ventilated area, spray one outside cover with spray adhesive. Attach the batting or felt and repeat for the spine and back cover. Don't pull the felt over the cover too tightly – make sure the album closes. Trim edges flush.

5 Lay the open album on the outer cover fabric. Measure and mark 5cm (2in) from all edges and cut the fabric. From the same fabric, cut two strips the length of the metal spine and 7.6cm (3in) wide. Fold over 6mm (¼in) on one long edge of each strip and press. Spray glue on the back of each strip and slide the folded edge under each side of the spine (use a butter knife to help).

6 Using the fabric for the inside cover, cut two pieces 2.5cm (1in) larger than the card all around. Spray glue on one side of each piece of the cut card. Place the fabric on the glued card leaving 2.5cm (1in)

of fabric all around. Turn the edges to the back of the card and glue using permanent fabric glue.

7 Centre the open album on the outside cover fabric. Turn all the edges to the inside and glue, starting with the centre of each edge, leaving the corners and 7.6cm (3in) from the spine free. Carefully ease the corners to fit and then glue. At the top and bottom edges by the spine measure the fabric 1.25cm (½in) away from the fold in the album towards the outer edge and clip within 1.25cm (½in) of the top edge. Fold the fabric under between the two cuts and tuck the folded edge behind the top edge of the metal spine and glue in place.

8 To assemble the album, cut the ribbon in half and centre one piece on each opening edge of the album at least 5cm (2in) in towards the centre. Glue in place. Carefully glue the back of the covered card close to the edge. Centre and attach this to the inside covers, making sure the fold on the inside of the album is free to close.

9 Centre the embroidery on the cover and glue in place, taking care no glue oozes out. Draw a thin bead of glue around the edge of the embroidery starting and ending at centre bottom. Attach the trim, gluing on a button where the raw ends meet.

Kiss the Cook Trivet

Stitch count 41h x 41w
Design size 7.6 x 7.6cm (3 x 3in)

Protect the surface of your table with this colourful trivet and remind everyone that all good cooks deserve appreciation. You can co-ordinate the trivet with your covered recipe book or the colour of your kitchen. You will need: a 15.2 x 15.2cm (6 x 6in) acrylic trivet (see Suppliers); a piece of heavy card cut to the same size as the opening; fabric glue; iron-on interfacing and decorative trim. Work on antique white 14-count Aida, following the instructions in step 2 opposite, and using the chart on page 49.

To make up the trivet, cut a piece of fabric 2.5cm (1in) larger than the card all around. Spray glue on one side of the cut card. Place the fabric on the glued card leaving 2.5cm (1in) of fabric all around. Turn the edges to the back of the card and glue using permanent fabric glue.

Cut iron-on interfacing 2.5cm (1in) larger than the embroidery all around. With the wrong side facing, centre the interfacing and fuse it to the embroidery. Trim to five rows beyond the design.

Centre the embroidery on the covered card and glue in place, taking care that no glue oozes out. Draw a thin bead of glue around the edge of the embroidery starting and ending at centre bottom and attach the trim. Mount the embroidery into the trivet and attach the backing.

Domestic Angels

43

Do-it-Yourself Angel Picture

Do you like to get things done even if it means doing it yourself? You'll feel well guided by this clever angel – after all, she's just like you, ready to handle just about anything!

Stitch count
103h x 131w

Design size
19 x 24cm (7½ x 9½in)

Go Shop!
- 37 x 32cm (14½ x 12½in) antique white 14-count Aida
- Tapestry needle size 24 and a beading needle
- Kreinik #4 Very Fine Braid 025 grey
- DMC stranded cotton (floss) as listed in chart key
- Mill Hill™ glass seed beads 03007 silver moon

1 Prepare for work, referring to page 100 if necessary. Find and mark the centre of the fabric and the centre of the chart on pages 52–53. Mount your fabric in an embroidery frame if you wish.

2 Start stitching from the centre of the chart, using two strands of stranded cotton for cross stitches. Use one strand for Kreinik #4 braid cross stitches and backstitches. Work all other backstitches with one strand. Following the chart for colour changes, work all French knots using one strand wrapped twice around the needle. Using a beading needle and matching thread, attach the beads (see page 101) according to the positions shown on the chart.

3 Once all the stitching is complete, finish your picture by mounting and framing (see page 102).

Fix-it-Chick Notebook

Stitch count 41h x 41w
Design size 7.6 x 7.6cm (3 x 3in)

Sometimes it's just easier to do things yourself, so join the club and declare yourself an official 'Fix-it-Chick'! A brightly decorated journal will help you keep track of supplies, plan out a project or tally expenses. You will need: a small book about 21 x 14cm (8¼ x 5½in); iron-on interfacing; permanent fabric glue; 0.5m (½yd) decorative trim and a decorative button. Work on antique white 14-count Aida following step 2 above, and use the chart on page 49.

To decorate the book cover, cut iron-on interfacing 2.5cm (1in) larger than the finished embroidery all around. With the wrong side facing, centre the interfacing and fuse to the embroidery. Trim to five rows beyond the design. Centre the embroidery at the top of the cover and fix with fabric glue. Glue the decorative trim along the raw edge of the embroidery starting and ending at centre bottom, attaching a button where ends meet.

Stitching Angel Cushion

We all know that stitchers are heaven sent and this charming angel comes complete with essential bits and bobs. This cushion would make a lovely gift to yourself or an equally talented friend.

Stitch count
103h x 131w

Design size
19 x 24cm (7½ x 9½in)

Go Shop!

- 32 x 37cm (12½ x 14½in) antique white 14-count Aida
- Tapestry needle size 24 and a beading needle
- Kreinik #4 Very Fine Braid 028 citron
- DMC stranded cotton (floss) as listed in chart key
- Mill Hill™ glass seed beads 00557 gold
- Background fabric 0.5m (½yd)
- Matching sewing thread
- Lightweight iron-on interfacing 0.25m (¼yd)
- Fusible web 0.25m (¼yd)
- 1.2m (1¼yd) decorative trim to tone with embroidery
- One decorative button
- Permanent fabric glue
- Polyester stuffing

1 Prepare for work, referring to page 100 if necessary. Find and mark the centre of the fabric and the centre of the chart on pages 54–55. Mount your fabric in an embroidery frame if you wish.

2 Start stitching from the centre of the chart, using two strands of stranded cotton (floss) for cross stitches. Use one strand to stitch all Kreinik #4 braid cross stitches and backstitches. Work all other backstitches with one strand. Following the chart for colour changes, work all French knots using one strand wrapped twice around the needle. Using a beading needle and matching thread, attach the beads (see page 101) according to the positions shown on the chart.

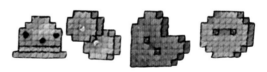

3 Once the stitching is complete, make up the cushion as follows. Place two 34.3 x 39.4cm (13½ x 15½in) pieces of background fabric right sides facing and sew a 1.25cm (½in) seam all around, leaving a generous opening at the bottom for turning. Turn right side out and press.

4 Cut a piece of lightweight interfacing 2.5cm (1in) larger than the finished embroidery all around and fuse it to the wrong side of the embroidery following the manufacturer's instructions. Trim the finished embroidery to within seven rows of the border edge. Cut a piece of fusible web to this size and place it on the wrong side of the embroidery, making sure that the edges do not overlap the trimmed embroidery. Centre your work on the prepared background. Press to fuse the embroidery and background fabric together.

5 Glue the decorative trim carefully around the outer edge of the embroidery, beginning and ending at centre bottom. Attach a decorative button where the ends meet. Stuff the cushion with polyester filling and slipstitch the bottom seam closed.

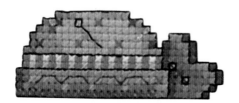

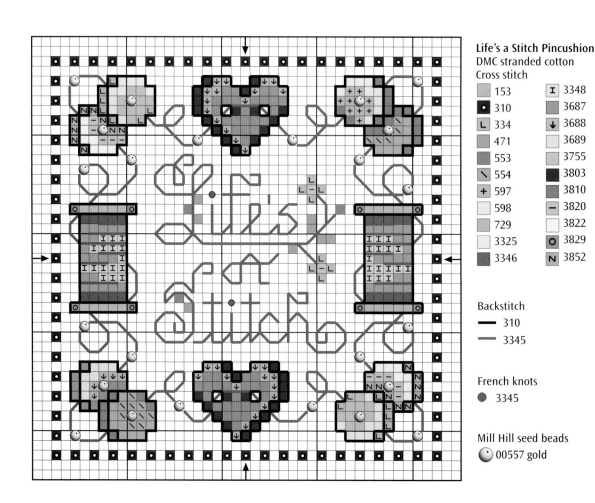

Life's a Stitch Pincushion

Stitch count 41h x 41w

Design size 7.6 x 7.6cm (3 x 3in)

Quick to work up and easy to assemble, this pincushion would make a lovely gift for a fellow cross stitch enthusiast. You will need: two 20.3cm (8in) squares of antique white 14-count Aida and a small bit of polyester filling. Follow the stitching instructions in step 2 on page 46 and use the chart below.

Make up the pincushion as follows. Trim the fabric to within 2.5cm (1in) of the finished embroidery. Using one strand of stranded cotton DMC 553, stitch a running stitch three rows beyond the last row of the embroidery, making the pincushion 47 x 47 stitches. Repeat this running stitch around a 47 x 47 stitch area on the blank Aida.

Trim both pieces of fabric to within six rows of the running stitch and fold along this line of stitches. Finger press in place, mitring the corners. With wrong sides together, use two strands of matching stranded cotton to whip stitch the running stitches from both pieces, starting at centre bottom. As you go, add a gold bead to every other stitch. Before finishing, stuff with polyester filling. Finish whip stitching until all edges are sealed.

Life's a Stitch Pincushion
DMC stranded cotton
Cross stitch

	153	I	3348
•	310		3687
L	334	↓	3688
	471		3689
	553		3755
\	554		3803
+	597		3810
	598	−	3820
	729		3822
	3325	O	3829
	3346	N	3852

Backstitch

— 310

— 3345

French knots

● 3345

Mill Hill seed beads

◯ 00557 gold

Domestic Angels

48

Kiss the Cook Trivet
DMC stranded cotton
Cross stitch

⊡	310	▧	801
	312		817
L	334		906
+	350		907
	351		3755
	434	–	3820
N	435		3822
>	676		3829
	729		

Backstitch
— 310
— 817

French knots
● 310

Mill Hill seed beads
◉ 02038 brilliant
    copper

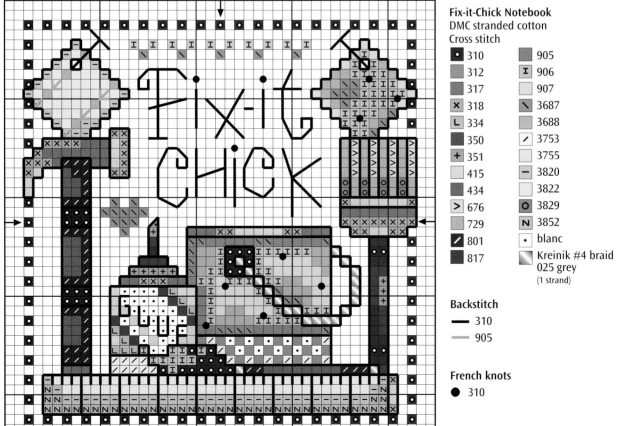

Fix-it-Chick Notebook
DMC stranded cotton
Cross stitch

⊡	310		905
	312	I	906
	317		907
✕	318	◥	3687
L	334		3688
	350	╱	3753
+	351		3755
	415	–	3820
	434		3822
>	676	O	3829
	729	N	3852
▧	801	·	blanc
	817	▨	Kreinik #4 braid
			025 grey
			(1 strand)

Backstitch
— 310
— 905

French knots
● 310

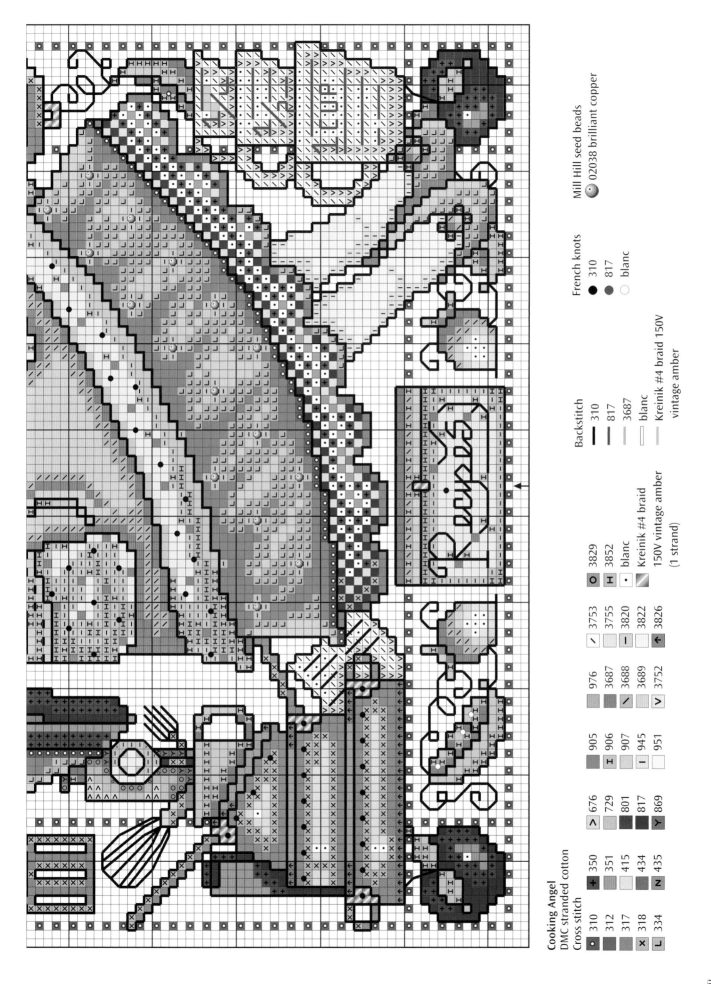

Cooking Angel
DMC stranded cotton
Cross stitch

·	310
■	312
■	317
■	318
✕	334
L	

+	350
■	351
■	415
■	434
N	435

⋋	676
■	729
■	801
■	817
Y	869

■	905
H	906
⁄	907
I	945
	951

╲	3753
■	3755
I	3820
■	3822
←	3826

■	976
■	3687
⁄	3688
■	3689
V	3752

O	3829
■	3852
·	blanc
⁄	Kreinik #4 braid
	150V vintage amber (1 strand)

Backstitch

— 310
— 817
— 3687
□ blanc
— Kreinik #4 braid 150V vintage amber

French knots

● 310
● 817
○ blanc

Mill Hill seed beads

◉ 02038 brilliant copper

51

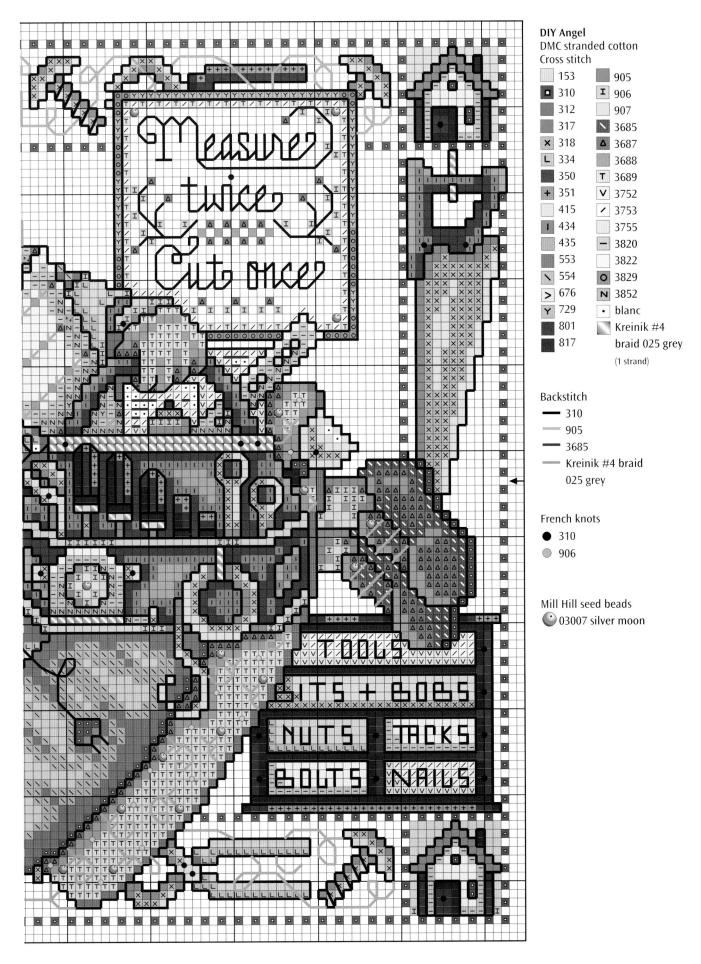

DIY Angel
DMC stranded cotton
Cross stitch

153		905	
310		906	I
312		907	
317		3685	
318	×	3687	Δ
334	L	3688	
350		3689	T
351	+	3752	V
415		3753	⁄
434	I	3755	
435		3820	–
553		3822	
554		3829	O
676	>	3852	N
729	Y	blanc	·
801		Kreinik #4	
817		braid 025 grey	
		(1 strand)	

Backstitch
— 310
— 905
— 3685
— Kreinik #4 braid
025 grey

French knots
● 310
○ 906

Mill Hill seed beads
03007 silver moon

Stitching Angel
DMC stranded cotton
Cross stitch

▨	153	▨	3346
⊙	310	I	3348
✕	318	▨	3687
L	334	↓	3688
▨	415	▨	3689
▨	471	V	3752
▨	553	╱	3753
╲	554	▨	3755
+	597	▨	3803
▨	598	▨	3810
>	676	−	3820
Y	729	▨	3822
T	762	O	3829
▨	869	N	3852
I	945	•	blanc
▨	951	▨	Kreinik #4 braid 028 citron (1 strand)
▨	3325		

Backstitch
— 310
— 3345
— 3803
— Kreinik #4 braid 028 citron

French knots
● 310
● 3345

Mill Hill seed beads
◉ 00557 gold

55

The Art of Ageing Gracefully

There was a time when women 'of a certain age' were expected to act in certain ways, perhaps to fade out of the spotlight a little. Today the world is our oyster and the possibilities for a rich and active life are endless.

Two fun notices are testimony to our youthful spirit and help us approach ageing with a smile on our faces. While we all realize that ageing is inevitable, let's make the most of it and be proud to show off our wisdom and experience with grace and humour. Through it all we can laugh at the numbers, no matter how many candles might be crowding our birthday cake. Fire up your energy anyway you please – be it with a brisk walk through the park or an invigorating bicycle ride along a country road.

There are also two designs that have been made up into great gifts – a slim case for storing photos of your latest adventures and a pretty make-up case to fit neatly into your handbag.

Ageing Gracefully Pictures

Whether it's that first wiry grey hair that seems to appear out of nowhere or your first pair of reading glasses, these pictures and accessories will help everyone look to the lighter side of ageing.

Stitch count (each design)
97h x 69w

Design size (each design)
17.5 x 12.5cm (7 x 5in)

Go Shop!
- 30.5 x 25.4cm (12 x 10in)
  14-count Aida
- Tapestry needle size 24
- DMC stranded cotton (floss)
  as listed in chart key

A WOMAN'S WIT. . .
*Age is a very high price
to pay for maturity.*

1 Prepare for work, referring to page 100 if necessary. Mark the centre of the fabric and chart on page 62 or 63. Mount your fabric in an embroidery frame if you wish.

2 Start stitching from the centre of chart and fabric. Use two strands of stranded cotton for full and three-quarter cross stitches. Work French knots using two strands wound once around the needle. Use one strand for backstitches.

3 Once stitching is complete, mount and frame your picture (see page 102) or make up in another way of your choice.

Gravity may take over our bodies but let's keep our hearts forever young. This charming slip case can be made up quickly using either Ultrasuede® fabric or felt (instructions overleaf) and tucks easily into your purse so you can show off your latest photos. There's also a useful make-up case (picture and instructions on page 61), to help you keep your looks *and* your sense of humour as the years advance.

Young at Heart Photo Case

It's always fun keeping a record of our lives through photographs. Stitch up this lovely slipcase to hold and show off the sweetest of the bunch.

Stitch count
69h x 97w
Design size
9.6 x 13.6cm (3¾ x 5½in)

Go Shop!
- 23 x 28cm (9 x 11in) 18-count white Aida
- Tapestry needle size 24 and a beading needle
- DMC stranded cotton (floss) as listed in chart key
- Mill Hill glass seed beads 02024 heather mauve
- 20.3 x 46cm (8 x 18in) Ultrasuede® to tone with embroidery for backing
- Lightweight iron-on interfacing and fusible web
- 60.9cm (24in) length of decorative trim to tone
- 30.5cm (12in) of 6mm (¼in) wide ribbon to tone
- One decorative button
- Permanent fabric glue
- 10 x 15.2cm (4 x 6in) ready-made photo pages (from stationery and craft shops)

A WOMAN'S WIT. . .
*I finally got my head together
but now my body is falling apart.*

1 Stitch the design following steps 1 and 2 on page 58.

2 Now make up the photo case as follows. Cut a piece of iron-on interfacing 2.5cm (1in) larger all round than the embroidery and fuse to the wrong side according to the manufacturer's instructions. Trim the embroidery to within four rows of the stitched border.

3 Fold the piece of Ultrasuede in half lengthways and press to crease. Lay the fabric flat, fold the two ends towards the centre crease by 10cm (4in) and tack (baste) in place. Using a 1.25cm (½in) seam, stitch the unfolded edges with matching sewing thread. Use pinking shears to pink the edges of the sewn sides.

4 Fold the stitched case in half, pockets on the inside. Cut a piece of fusible web the size of the trimmed embroidery. Centre the embroidery on the outside of the folded case, sandwiching the web between the case and the wrong side of the embroidery. Press to fuse. Using a thin line of fabric glue, attach the decorative trim around the edge of the trimmed embroidery, beginning and ending at centre bottom. Cut the length of ribbon in half and glue it to the case where the trim ends meet, attaching a small button to hide raw ends. At the centre of the back edge, attach the other half of the ribbon by turning over 1.25cm (½in) and gluing in place. To finish, slip the photo pages into the inside pocket of the case and tie the ribbons together.

Mirror, Mirror Cosmetics Case

Sometimes the reflection we see in the mirror can surprise us! Reach into this handy cosmetics case when it's time for a bit of blush or a dash of lipstick to brighten your spirits.

Stitch count
69h x 97w

Design size
9.6 x 13.6cm (3¾ x 5½in)

Go Shop!

- 23 x 28cm (9 x 11in) 18-count white Aida
- Tapestry needle size 24 and a beading needle
- DMC stranded cotton (floss) as listed in chart key
- Mill Hill glass seed beads 02031 citron
- 20.3 x 46cm (8 x 18in) Ultrasuede® to tone with embroidery
- 19 x 33cm (7½ x 13in) fabric for lining
- Lightweight iron-on interfacing and fusible web
- 61cm (24in) length of decorative trim to tone
- 38cm (15in) of 6mm (¼in) wide ribbon to tone
- Two decorative buttons
- Permanent fabric glue

1 Stitch the design following steps 1 and 2 on page 58 and then make up the cosmetics case as follows.

2 Cut a piece of iron-on interfacing 2.5cm (1in) larger all round than the embroidery and fuse to the wrong side. Trim the embroidery to within four rows of the stitched border. Cut iron-on interfacing the same size as the lining fabric and fuse to the wrong side of the fabric. Cut fusible web the same size as the prepared lining. Centre the lining right side facing on the wrong side of the Ultrasuede and sandwich the fusible web between. Press to fuse. Fold the top and bottom edges towards the lining by 1.25cm (½in). Press the folds and glue in place. Fold the Ultrasuede 13.3cm (5¼in) up from the bottom and 8.9cm (3½in) down from the top and crease. Open up the top flap and stitch side seams together with matching sewing thread using 1.25cm (½in) seams. Pink the edges.

3 Cut fusible web the size of the trimmed embroidery. Centre the embroidery on the front of the folded case, sandwiching the web between the case and the wrong side of the embroidery. Press to fuse. Using a thin line of glue, attach the trim around the edge of the embroidery, beginning and ending at centre bottom. Cut the ribbon in half and glue both ends to the front of the case where the trim ends meet, attaching a button to hide raw ends. Attach the other button at the centre of the top back flap. Bring the ribbon ends to the back and tie round the button to close.

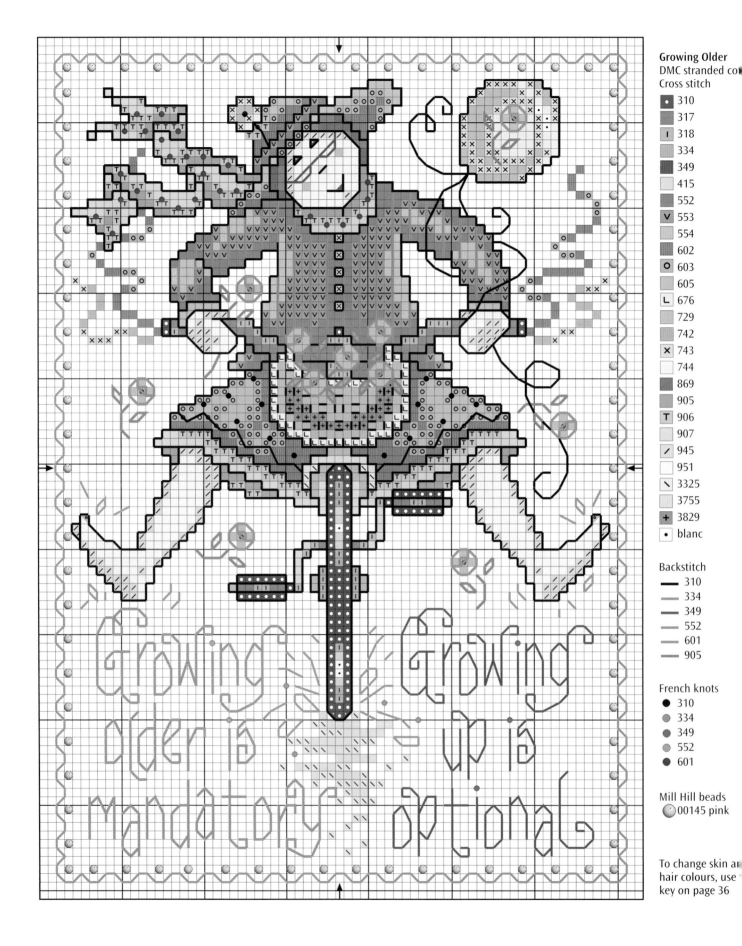

Growing Older

DMC stranded co[tton]
Cross stitch

⊡	310
	317
I	318
	334
	349
	415
	552
V	553
	554
	602
O	603
	605
L	676
	729
	742
X	743
	744
	869
	905
T	906
	907
╱	945
	951
╲	3325
	3755
+	3829
•	blanc

Backstitch
— 310
— 334
— 349
— 552
— 601
— 905

French knots
● 310
● 334
● 349
● 552
● 601

Mill Hill beads
◯ 00145 pink

To change skin a[nd]
hair colours, use
key on page 36

So Many Candles
DMC stranded cotton
Cross stitch

☒	310
	334
	349
↓	350
	552
V	553
	554
	602
O	603
	605
L	676
	729
	742
✕	743
	744
	869
	905
T	906
	907
╱	945
	951
╲	3325
	3755
✚	3829
•	blanc

Backstitch
— 310
— 312
— 552
┅ 601
— 905

French knots
● 310
● 312
● 552

Mill Hill beads
⊙ 02031 citron

To change skin and hair colours, use the key on page 36

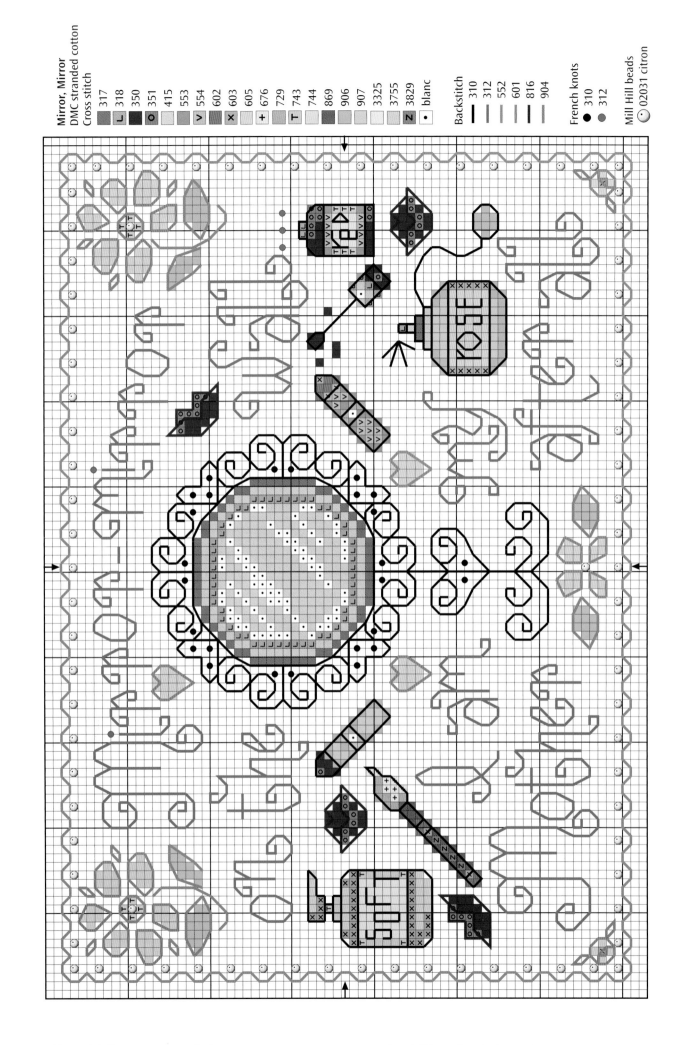

Mirror, Mirror
DMC stranded cotton
Cross stitch

	317
⌐	318
	350
O	351
	415
∨	553
	554
✕	602
+	603
	605
	676
	729
T	743
	744
	869
	906
	907
	3325
	3755
Z	3829
•	blanc

Backstitch
	310
	312
	552
	601
	816
	904

French knots
● 310
● 312

Mill Hill beads
⊙ 02031 citron

Young at Heart
DMC stranded cotton
Cross stitch

| 603 |
| 605 |
| 906 |
| 3325 |
| < 3755 |

Backstitch
312
322
552
601
904

French knots
● 552
● 742

Mill Hill beads
● 02024
  heather mauve

Victorian Lady's Garden

Women have always been adept at communication and during the Victorian era the language of flowers became a subtle form of communication between the sexes. Small bouquets known as tussie-mussies, wrapped in delicate lace doilies and satin ribbon were sent to speak secret words of love that dare not be spoken aloud. A young woman presented with one of these bouquets that included a note of invitation to a dance would accept by returning one of the flowers in an upright position to the sender. Entire dictionaries were written listing specific flowers and their meanings. Love, grace, faithfulness, purity and hope were but a few of the messages conveyed.

Surrounded by a Victorian stencil-style border, these lovely flowers and their hidden meanings present a sampling of the finest attributes of the 'fairer sex'. Fragrant lilies, delicate violets and opulent ranunculus pay homage to every woman.

You can use any of the flowers from the main chart to make a whole range of pretty projects – see overleaf for ideas that include a trinket pot, greetings card and little pillow.

Victorian Garden Picture

Flowers are gifts that have always charmed and fascinated the woman who receives them and, like a woman, they possess qualities that symbolize, love, romance and the feminine mystique.

Stitch count
213h x 157w

Design size
38.6 x 28.5cm (15¼ x 11¼in)

Go Shop!
✦50.8 x 40.6cm (20 x 16in) antique white 28-count Monaco (Charles Craft code 0322)
✦Tapestry needle size 24
✦DMC stranded cotton (floss) as listed in chart key

1 Prepare for work, referring to page 100 if necessary. Mark the centre of the fabric and chart (pages 70–73). Use an embroidery frame if you wish.

2 Start stitching from the centre of chart and fabric, working over two threads. Use two strands of stranded cotton for full and three-quarter cross stitches. Work French knots using two strands wound once around the needle. Use one strand for backstitches and long stitches.

3 Once stitching is complete, mount and frame your picture (see page 102).

Primrose Trinket Pot

Stitch count 41h x 39w
Design size 7.6 x 7cm (3 x 2¾in)

This flower is the symbol of the hope and promise of early youth, so stitch it for a special young lady. You will need: 20.3cm (8in) square of putty 28-count Cashel linen (Zweigart code 345) and a trinket pot (Framecraft W4E). Stitch the motif on page 70/71 following the stitching instructions in step 2 above. Mount your embroidery in the pot lid according to the manufacturer's instructions.

Violet Card

Stitch count 32h x 28w
Design size 5.8 x 5cm (2¼ x 2in)

Every spring the front lawn of my Vermont home is a sea of sweetly scented blue violets. With their appearance year after year I see why they have been assigned the quality of faithfulness. Make up this card for some one you'll always cherish. You will need: 20.3cm (8in) square of mint green 28-count Jubilee linen (Zweigart code 621) and a card mount. Stitch the motif on page 72/73 following the stitching instructions in step 2 above. Mount your embroidery in the card (see page 101) and add a bow.

Rose Pillow

No flower represents a woman quite like the rose. Make up this beautiful sachet pillow and fill it with dried rose petals if you like. What a lovely way to freshen your day.

Stitch count
71h x 52w
Design size
12.7 x 8.9cm (5 x 3½in)

Go Shop!
- 25.4 x 23cm (10 x 9in) barely blue 28-count Jobelan
- Tapestry needle size 24
- DMC stranded cotton (floss) as listed in chart key
- 20.3 x 25.4cm (8 x 10in) piece of fabric for backing
- Lightweight iron-on interfacing
- 0.5m (½yd) length of 6mm (¼in) wide ribbon
- 0.5m (½yd) length of 2.5cm (1in) wide decorative lace
- Permanent fabric glue
- Polyester stuffing

1 Prepare for work and stitch the flower motif following step 2 opposite.

2 Make up into a sachet pillow as follows. Cut a 20.3 x 25.4cm (8 x 10in) piece of iron-on interfacing. With the wrong side of your work facing, centre the interfacing and fuse to the embroidery. Trim the embroidery 6.5cm (2½in) from the sides and 3.8cm (1½in) from the top and bottom beyond the design.

3 Cut the lengths of ribbon and lace in half. Glue the lace 2.5cm (1in) from either side of the stitching. Glue the ribbon at the inside edge of each piece of lace. Trim to match raw edges at top and bottom. Cut backing fabric to the same size as the trimmed embroidery, right sides facing, and pin in place. Using matching thread, stitch a 1.25cm (½in) seam all around, leaving an opening at the bottom. Turn through to the right side and stuff with polyester filling. Slipstitch the bottom opening closed.

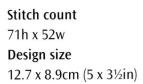

A WOMAN'S WIT...
Women are the flowers in life's garden.

Victorian Garden
DMC stranded
cotton Cross stitch

▨	208
V	209
▫	211
⊡	311
▨	312
＼	322
▨	340
L	341
◼	349
↓	351
Y	352
▨	470
T	471
–	676
▫	677
×	726
▨	727
▨	729
▨	741
N	742
I	746
◼	817
O	819
◼	938
▨	961
▫	963
▨	986
+	987
▨	989
∧	3078
L	3350
／	3716
▨	3746
◉	3803
▨	3829
•	blanc

Backstitch

——	311
——	938
——	986

French knots

●	311
●	470
●	938
○	3078

Hope

Beauty

Dignity

Bottom left

Victorian Garden
DMC stranded
cotton Cross stitch

▨	208
V	209
▦	211
⊙	311
▨	312
\	322
▦	340
L	341
■	349
↓	351
Y	352
▨	470
T	471
−	676
	677
×	726
	727
▦	729
▨	741
N	742
I	746
■	817
O	819
■	938
▨	961
▦	963
▨	986
+	987
▦	989
∧	3078
L	3350
/	3716
▨	3746
◎	3803
▨	3829
•	blanc

Backstitch
───	311
───	938
───	986

French knots
●	311
●	470
●	938
○	3078

Bottom right

73

Sweet Indulgence

There are times when you just have to throw caution to the wind and let loose. With so many do's and don'ts in life, a little sweet indulgence every once in a while can't really hurt. In fine form and with tongue firmly planted in cheek, these four bodacious bovines let it all hang out. If achieving the perfect body seems just beyond your reach, slip into something slinky, get out that feather boa, strike a pose and be proud of what you have. No matter how itsy-bitsy your bikini is, a holiday is no time to start counting calories, so relax and enjoy yourself – there will be plenty of time back home for getting on the scales to engage in some 'wishful shrinking'. Last but not least, we all know the temptations of chocolate,

but let's face it, it is simply irresistible!

To help carry on the sweet life there are two matching fridge magnets to stitch and make up – perfect trinkets for a fellow calorie counter.

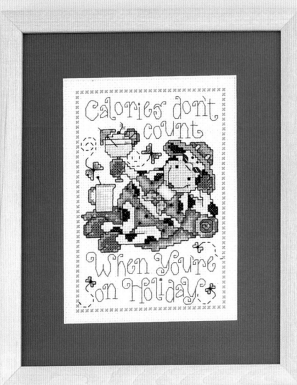

Calories don't count When You're on Holiday.

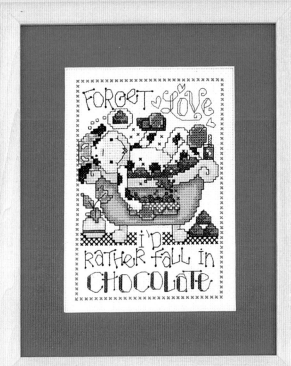

FORGET LOVE I'D RATHER FALL IN CHOCOLATE

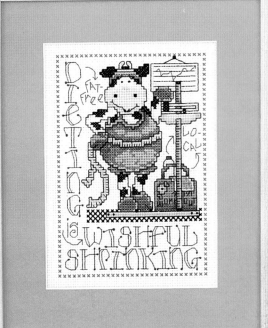

DIETING FAT-FREE LO-CAL is WISHFUL SHRINKING

Having a perfect body isn't difficult IT'S IMPOSSIBLE!

Sweet Life Pictures

Life's too short to be watching your waistline 24/7. Treat yourself to a bit of indulgence every once in a while. You can always take an extra lap around the block tomorrow.

Stitch count (each picture)
89h x 61w
Design size (each picture)
16.5 x 11.4cm (6½ x 4½in)

Go Shop!
30.5 x 25.5cm (12 x 10in)
14-count natural Aida
Tapestry needle size 24
DMC stranded cotton (floss)
as listed in chart key

1 Prepare for work, referring to page 100 if necessary. Mark the centre of the fabric and centre of the chart on pages 78–81. Mount your fabric in an embroidery frame if you wish.

2 Start stitching from the centre of the chart and fabric. Use two strands of stranded cotton (floss) for full and three-quarter cross stitches. Work all French knots using two strands wound once around the needle. Following the chart colours, use one strand for backstitches and long stitches.

3 Once all the stitching is complete, finish your picture by mounting and framing (see page 102).

Fridge Magnets

Stitch count (each design) 43h x 43w
Design size 7.6 x 7.6cm (3 x 3in)

These colourful magnets may not keep you from opening the fridge but they are sure to bring a smile to your day. For each magnet you will need: 20.3cm (8in) square of natural 14-count Aida; two 10cm (4in) squares of felt; lightweight iron-on interfacing and fusible web and 25.4 x 30.5cm (10 x 12in) self-adhesive photo magnet sheet (from craft and stationery shops). Follow the charts opposite, using the stitching instructions in step 2 above. Make up a magnet by following the instructions on page 102.

A WOMAN'S WIT. . .
*Eat, drink, and be merry,
for tomorrow we diet!*

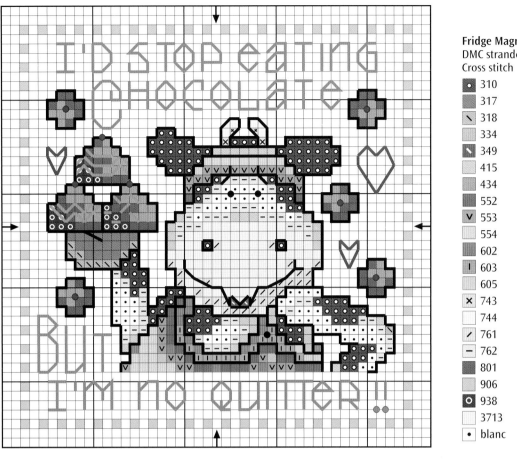

Fridge Magnets
DMC stranded cotton
Cross stitch

⊙	310
	317
\	318
	334
\	349
	415
	434
	552
V	553
	554
	602
I	603
	605
×	743
	744
∕	761
–	762
	801
	906
⊙	938
	3713
•	blanc

Backstitch
──	310
──	312
──	349
⋯	602

French knots
●	310
●	312
●	349

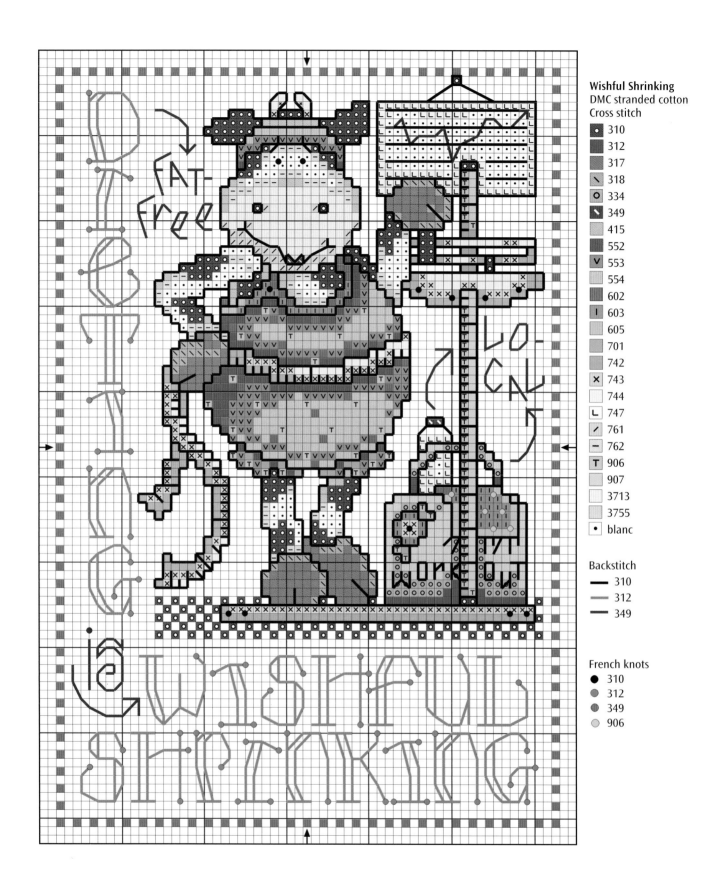

Wishful Shrinking
DMC stranded cotton
Cross stitch

◉	310
	312
	317
\	318
O	334
◣	349
	415
	552
V	553
	554
	602
I	603
	605
	701
	742
×	743
	744
L	747
╱	761
–	762
T	906
	907
	3713
	3755
•	blanc

Backstitch
— 310
— 312
— 349

French knots
● 310
● 312
● 349
○ 906

Calories Don't Count
DMC stranded cotton
Cross stitch

- ⊙ 310
- 317
- ＼ 318
- Ｏ 334
- ◣ 349
- 415
- 552
- V 553
- 554
- 602
- I 603
- 605
- 701
- 729
- 742
- × 743
- 744
- L 747
- ╱ 761
- − 762
- T 906
- 907
- + 3325
- 3713
- 3755
- I 3829
- • blanc

Backstitch
- —— 310
- —— 349
- ═══ blanc

French knots
- ● 310
- ● 349
- ● 602

Forget Love
DMC stranded cotton
Cross stitch

⊙	310
	317
\	318
⊙	334
\	349
	415
	434
	602
I	603
	605
	701
	742
×	743
	744
L	747
/	761
–	762
	801
T	906
	907
⊙	938
	3713
•	blanc

Backstitch

— 310
— 349
— 602
— 801

French knots

● 310
● 349
● 801
○ 906

Having a
Perfect Body
DMC stranded cotton
Cross stitch

- 310
- 317
- 318
- 349
- 351
- 415
- 552
- 602
- 603
- 605
- 701
- 742
- 743
- 744
- 761
- 762
- 906
- 907
- 3713
- blanc

Backstitch
— 310
— 312

French knots
- 310
- 312

For All the Women I Am

Women take on so many important roles and provide love and comfort that comes from the heart. We all take our places, be it as a mother, daughter, sister, aunt, wife or grandmother. Each woman guides and teaches in some way, old to young, child to adult. One shines light on the other through unique experiences, while shared love guides and strengthens us along the way. I think of the time when as a child I sat by my grandmother as she told me about her voyage to America when she was young and all that it meant to her. I think too of a day not so long ago when I looked out on the lawn after fresh rain and saw my young niece twirling beneath a full rainbow shouting the word 'happy' through a big smile.

I've designed the four loving sentiments in this chapter to honour the part that each and every woman plays within her family. Indeed, we owe it to ourselves to take the time to stop and notice how gratifying it can be to know that we, as women, can touch the life of another person in so many meaningful ways.

Mothers Wall Hanging

The love between mother and child is a love that is never ending. Long after a child ventures out into the world, we feel the loving comfort of our mother's heart always with us.

Stitch count
110h x 63w
Design size
20 x 11.5cm (8 x 4½in)

Go Shop!
- 33 x 25.4cm (13 x 10in) 28-count antique white Monaco (Charles Craft code 0322)
- Tapestry needle size 24
- DMC stranded cotton (floss) as listed in chart key
- 23 x 15.2cm (9 x 6in) white felt for backing
- Lightweight interfacing and fusible web
- Tassel to tone with embroidery
- Permanent fabric glue
- 30.5cm (12in) length of 6mm (¼in) wide blue ribbon
- 12.7cm (5in) long white wooden bell pull (see Suppliers)

A WOMAN'S WIT. . .
Mother is another name for Love

1 Prepare for work, referring to page 100 if necessary. Mark the centre of the fabric and chart (page 88).

2 Start stitching from the centre of the chart and fabric and work over two fabric threads. Use two strands of stranded cotton (floss) for cross stitches. Work French knots using two strands wound once around the needle. Use one strand for backstitches.

3 Once stitching is complete, make up the hanging as follows. Draw a cutting line in pencil along the sides and bottom edges 2.5cm (1in) beyond the design. Draw a line 5.7cm (2¼in) beyond the top edge of the embroidery. Cut interfacing 2.5cm (1in) larger than the marked lines. Centre it on the wrong side of the embroidery and fuse according to the manufacturer's instructions. Cut the shape along the pencil lines.

4 Fold the sides and bottom edges to the back leaving 1.25cm (½in) beyond the embroidery and a point at the bottom. Press and glue in place. Fold the top raw edge under by 1.25cm (½in), press and glue in place. Fold back the top by 2.5cm (1in) and press. Cut the felt backing and fusible web 6mm (¼in) smaller than the shape all around. Sandwich the web between the wrong side of the embroidery and the felt, tucking both under the top fold-over. Press to fuse. Make a small stitch where the folded edge meets the back of the hanging.

5 Insert the bell pull dowel through the fold. Cut the ribbon in half and attach to the pull by making a loop and gluing each end in place. Tie in a bow for hanging. Make a tassel from matching threads (see page 103) or use a purchased tassel, and sew it to the bottom.

Grandmother Picture

I can still remember when my Nana held my tiny hand to cross the city streets on the way to get my favourite ice cream soda. Celebrate your special grandmum with this charming sampler.

Stitch count
69h x 97w

Design size
12.5 x 17.7cm (5 x 7in)

Go Shop!
✦ 25.4 x 30.5cm (10 x 12in)
  28-count antique white Monaco
  (Charles Craft code 0322)
✦ Tapestry needle size 24 and a
  beading needle
✦ DMC stranded cotton (floss)
  as listed in chart key
✦ Mill Hill glass seed beads
  00479 white

1 Prepare for work, marking the centre of the fabric and chart (page 89).

2 Start stitching from the centre of the chart and fabric, working over two fabric threads. Use two strands of stranded cotton (floss) for cross stitches. Work French knots using two strands wound once around the needle. Use one strand for backstitches. Attach beads (see page 101) using a beading needle and matching thread.

3 Use the charted alphabet and numbers to stitch the names of baby and grandmother and the birth date. Plan the letters on graph paper first to make sure they fit the space.

4 Once stitching is complete, mount and frame your picture (see page 102).

Sisters Photo Album

Sisters share adventures and memories through a bond that is especially unique. This elegant covered album (right) is the perfect place to store shared mementos and family photos.

Stitch count
91h x 63w
Design size
16.5 x 11.5cm (6½ x 4½in)

Go Shop!
+ 30.5 x 25.4cm (12 x 10in) barely blue 28-count Jobelan
+ Tapestry needle size 24 and a beading needle
+ DMC stranded cotton (floss) as listed in chart key
+ Mill Hill beads as listed in chart key
+ One standard three-ring photo album 29 x 25.4cm (11½ x 10in)
+ 0.5m (½yd) white felt or cotton batting
+ 0.5m (½yd) fabric for outside cover and 0.5m (½yd) fabric for inside cover, to tone with embroidery
+ Lightweight iron-on interfacing
+ Two pieces 28 x 24cm (11 x 9½in) heavy white card and one piece 23 x 17.8cm (9 x 7in)
+ Spray craft adhesive and permanent fabric glue

1 Prepare for work, marking the centre of the fabric and centre of the chart on page 90. Follow the stitching instructions in step 2, page 85.

2 Make up a covered photo album by following steps 3–7 on page 42, and continue as follows.

3 To create a frame for the embroidery, using the smaller piece of white card, measure and mark 2.5cm (1in) towards the centre from all sides. Cut out the centre rectangle with a sharp craft knife. Cut a 28 x 23cm (11 x 9in) piece of inside cover fabric. Spray the cut card frame with adhesive and glue to the wrong side of the fabric. Using sharp scissors, cut a diagonal slit from the centre of the empty rectangle to each corner. Fold the fabric to the back of the frame, trimming so it does not overlap the outer edges. Glue in place.

4 To assemble the album, cut the ribbon in half and centre one piece on each opening edge of the album at least 5cm (2in) in towards the centre. Glue in place. Glue the back of the inside cover card close to the edge. Centre and attach this to the inside covers making sure that the fold on the inside of the album is free to close. Centre the finished embroidery on the cover and glue in place. To finish, place the prepared fabric frame over the embroidery and glue in place.

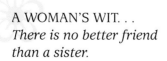

A WOMAN'S WIT. . .
There is no better friend than a sister.

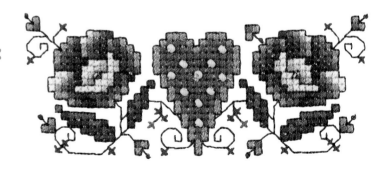

Daughters Keepsake Box

Stitch count 75h x 75w
Design size 13.6 x 13.6cm (5½ x 5½in)

No matter what role a woman takes on in the family, we are all someone's daughter. Make up this beautiful keepsake box for you own dear girl so as she grows she can fill it with small treasures she gathers over the years. You will need: 25.4cm (10in) square of mint green 28-count Jubilee (Zweigart code 621); Mill Hill white seed beads 00479 and a 15.2cm (6in) square wooden keepsake box (Sudberry House code 99531). Follow the chart on page 91, using the stitching instructions in step 2 on page 85. Mount your embroidery in the box according to the manufacturer's instructions.

Use this backstitch alphabet and numbers to change the names and dates on the chart

Grandmothers

DMC stranded cotton
Cross stitch

	676
·	677
+	729
⁄	869
■	938
▨	3829

Backstitch
— 869
— 938

French knots
○ 677
● 869
● 938

Mill Hill beads
◉ 00479 white

Sisters
DMC stranded cotton

Cross stitch

- 152
- 221
- T 223
- • 225
- 3721
- 3857

Backstitch

- 3857

French knots

- 225
- 3857

Mill Hill beads

- Antique 03018 coral reef
- Magnifica 10033 antique cranberry

Daughters
DMC stranded cotton
Cross stitch

·	818		3687
■	3685	＼	3688

	3689
V	3803

Backstitch
— 3685

French knots
○ 818
● 3685

Mill Hill beads
◉ 00479 white

Sea Goddess

Picture the sea on a late summer's afternoon: waning sunlight dazzles and flickers across the rolling waves; below the shimmering surface of the ocean lies a world of wonder and mystery. Playful seahorses and brilliant jewel-toned fish gather round to greet the Goddess of the Sea. With an outstretched hand, this lissome figure drifts freely amidst the plants and creatures of the deep in a nurturing and joyful dance. On her head she wears a seashell crown and tiny pearls float through her glorious tresses. A gossamer cape studded with delicate iridescent bubbles drifts across her shoulders. Sparkling metallic threads embroider her bodice and a sash of silver and pearls flows from her waist.

A beautiful hand-dyed evenweave has been chosen for stitching the sea goddess, which enhances the design but if you prefer the goddess could also be worked on one of the many lovely solid colours of evenweave or Aida that are available in your favourite needlework shop.

Sea Goddess Picture

If you dive deeply into the swirling waves of the sea you will discover what lies below. A radiant Sea Goddess lights up the dark waters with her graceful shimmering presence.

Stitch count
243h x 187w
Design size
44 x 34cm (17½ x 13½in)

Go Shop!
- 58.4 x 48.3cm (23 x 19in) neptune 28-count hand-dyed Jobelan (Polstitches – see Suppliers)
- Tapestry needle size 24 and a beading needle
- DMC stranded cotton (floss) as listed in chart key
- Kreinik #4 Very Fine Braid as listed in chart key
- Mill Hill glass seed beads as listed in chart key

1 Prepare for work, referring to page 100 if necessary. Mark the centre of the fabric and centre of the chart on pages 96–99. Mount your fabric in an embroidery frame if you wish.

2 Start stitching from the centre of the chart and fabric, using two strands of stranded cotton (floss) for full and three-quarter cross stitches. Work French knots using one strand wound twice around the needle. Use one strand to stitch all Kreinik #4 braid cross stitches and backstitches. Work all other backstitches with one strand of stranded cotton.

3 Using a beading needle and matching thread, attach the beads (see page 101) according to the positions shown on the chart.

4 Once all the stitching is complete, finish your picture by mounting and framing (see page 102) or display the design in some other way.

Carp Card and Seahorse Sachet

Stitch count (each project) 29h x 29w
Design size (each project) 5.3 x 5.3cm (2 x 2in)

Stitch a sweet little seahorse or jewel-coloured fish for a sachet or card. Each design was stitched on a 17.8cm (7in) square of neptune 28-count hand-dyed Opalescent Lugana (Polstitches – see Suppliers) but you could use a pale blue linen instead. The motifs are from the main chart but have been re-charted below to include a blue border. Use two strands of stranded cotton (floss) for full and three-quarter cross stitches. Work French knots using one strand wound twice around the needle. Use one strand to stitch all Kreinik #4 braid backstitches. Work all other backstitches with one strand. Attach beads with a beading needle and matching thread. Once all stitching is complete, mount the embroidery into a card (see page 101) or make up into a mini-sachet (see page 103).

A WOMAN'S WIT. . .
*Mother Nature is
never hasty, yet she
accomplishes everything.*

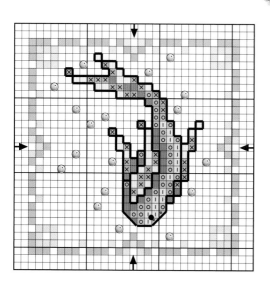

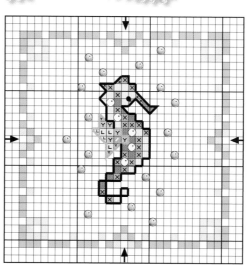

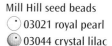

Carp and Seahorse
DMC stranded cotton
Cross stitch

■ 517	597
O 518	598
I 519	831
/ 562	✗ 833
Y 563	834
L 564	

Backstitch
— 3799
— Kreinik #4
braid 102 vatican

French knots
● 3799

Mill Hill seed beads
⊙ 03021 royal pearl
◉ 03044 crystal lilac

Sea Goddess

95

Sea Goddess
DMC stranded cotton
Cross stitch

⊡	310	▨	945
	320	◣	951
	340		975
	341		976
T	368	+	987
	471	╱	3347
	472		3687
	517		3688
O	518		3746
I	519	−	3747
╱	562		3770
Y	563		3799
L	564	◉	3809
	597	V	3811
	598		3826
	831	•	blanc
✕	833	▨	Kreinik #4
	834		braid 102 vatican (1 strand)

Backstitch

━━━ 975

━━━ 3799

━━━ Kreinik #4 braid
      102 vatican

━━━ Kreinik #4 braid
      684 aquamarine

━━━ Kreinik #4 braid
      3533 purple mambo

French knots

● 3799

Mill Hill seed beads

◉ 02070 sea mist

◉ 03021 royal pearl

◉ 03044 crystal lilac

Bottom left

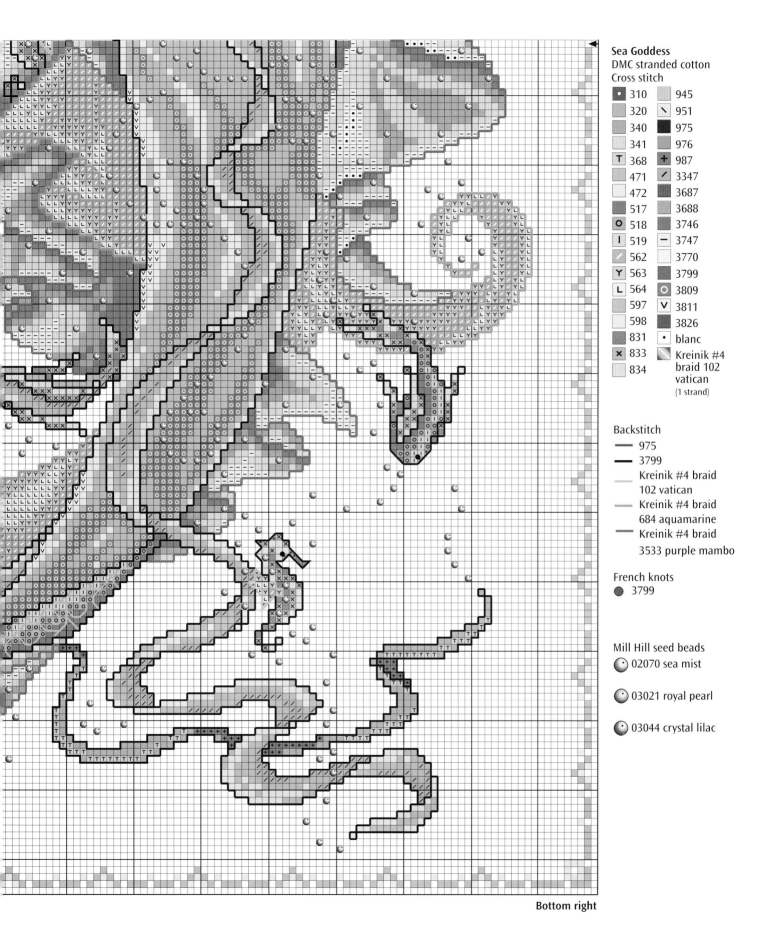

Sea Goddess
DMC stranded cotton
Cross stitch

⊙	310		945
	320	⬆	951
	340		975
	341	+	976
T	368	+	987
	471	/	3347
	472		3687
	517		3688
O	518		3746
I	519	−	3747
/	562		3770
Y	563		3799
L	564	O	3809
	597	V	3811
	598		3826
	831	•	blanc
✕	833	◩	Kreinik #4
	834		braid 102
			vatican
			(1 strand)

Backstitch

═══	975
▬▬▬	3799
	Kreinik #4 braid
	102 vatican
	Kreinik #4 braid
	684 aquamarine
	Kreinik #4 braid
	3533 purple mambo

French knots
● 3799

Mill Hill seed beads
⊙ 02070 sea mist

◔ 03021 royal pearl

◑ 03044 crystal lilac

Bottom right

99

Useful Information

This section describes the materials and equipment required, the basic techniques and stitches used and some general making up methods. Refer to Suppliers for useful addresses.

Materials

Fabrics
The designs have been worked mostly on a blockweave fabric called Aida. If you change the gauge (count) of the material, that is the number of holes per inch, then the size of the finished work will alter accordingly. Some of the designs have been stitched on evenweave and in this case need to be worked over two fabric threads instead of one block.

Threads
The projects have been stitched with DMC stranded embroidery cotton (floss) but you could match the colours to other thread ranges – ask at your local needlework store. The six-stranded skeins can easily be split into separate strands. The project instructions tell you how many strands to use. Some projects use Kreinik metallic thread for added glitter – use one strand for this thread.

Needles
Tapestry needles, available in different sizes, are used for cross stitch as they have a rounded point and do not snag fabric. You will need a thinner beading needle to attach the small glass seed beads used in some of the projects.

Frames
It is a matter of personal preference as to whether you use an embroidery frame to keep your fabric taut while stitching. Generally speaking, working with a frame helps to keep the tension even and prevent distortion, while working without a frame is faster and less cumbersome. Various frames are available – look in your local needlework store.

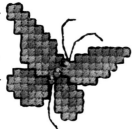

Techniques

Preparing the Fabric
Before starting work, check the design size given with each project and make sure that this is the size you require for your finished embroidery. Your fabric should be at least 5cm (2in) larger all the way round than the finished size of the stitching, to allow for making up. Before beginning to stitch, neaten the fabric edges either by hemming or zigzagging to prevent fraying as you work.

Finding the Fabric Centre
Marking the centre of the fabric is important regardless of which direction you work from, in order to stitch the design centrally on the fabric. To find the centre, fold the fabric in half horizontally and then vertically, then tack (baste) along the folds (or use tailor's chalk). The centre point is where the two lines of tacking (basting) meet. This point on the fabric should correspond to the centre point on the chart. Remove these lines on completion of the work.

Calculating Design Size
Each project gives the stitch count and finished design size but if you want to work the design on a different count fabric you will need to re-calculate the finished size. Count the number of stitches in each direction on the chart and then divide these numbers by the fabric count number, e.g., 140 x 140 ÷ 14-count = a design size of 10 x 10in (25.5 x 25.5cm). Working on evenweave usually means working over two fabric threads, so divide the fabric count by two before you start calculating.

Using Charts and Keys
The charts in this book are easy to work from. Each square represents one stitch. Each coloured square, or coloured square with a symbol, represents a thread colour, with the code number given in the chart key. A few of the designs use fractional stitches (three-quarter stitches) to give more definition. Solid coloured lines show where backstitches or long stitches are to be worked. French knots are shown by coloured circles. Larger coloured circles with a dot indicate beads.

Each complete chart has arrows at the sides to show the centre point, which you could mark with a pen. Where the charts have been split over several pages, the key is repeated. For your own use, you could colour photocopy and enlarge charts, taping the parts together.

Starting/Finishing Stitching
Avoid using knots when starting and finishing as this will make your work uneven and lumpy when mounted. Bring the needle up at the start of the first stitch, leaving a 2.5cm (1in) 'tail' at the back. Secure this tail by working the first few stitches over it. Start new threads by passing the needle through several stitches on the back of the work.

To finish off thread, pass the needle through several nearby stitches on the wrong side of the work, then cut the thread off close to the fabric.

Washing and Pressing
If you need to wash your finished embroidery, first make sure the stranded cottons are colourfast by washing them in tepid water and mild soap. Rinse well and lay out flat to dry completely before stitching. Wash completed embroideries in the same way. To iron embroidery, use a medium setting, covering the ironing board with a thick layer of towelling. Place the stitching right side down and press gently, taking extra care with glass seed beads and metallic threads.

The Stitches

Backstitch

Backstitches are used to give definition to parts of a design and to outline areas. Many of the charts use different coloured backstitches. Follow Fig 1, bringing the needle up at 1, down at 2, up again at 3, down at 4 and so on.

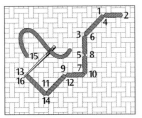

Fig 1
Working
backstitch

Cross Stitch

A cross stitch can be worked singly (Fig 2a) or half stitches can be sewn in a line and completed on the return journey (Fig 2b).

To make a cross stitch over one block of Aida, bring the needle up through the fabric at the bottom left side of the stitch (number 1 on Fig 2a) and cross diagonally to the top right corner (2). Push the needle through the hole and bring up through at 3, crossing the fabric diagonally to finish the stitch at 4. To work the next stitch, come up through the bottom right corner of the first stitch and repeat the sequence.

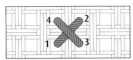

Fig 2a
Working
a single
cross stitch

To work a line of cross stitches, stitch the first part of the stitch as above and repeat these half cross stitches along the row. Complete the crosses on the way back. Note: for neat work, always finish the cross stitch with the top stitches lying in the same diagonal direction.

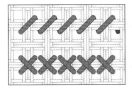

Fig 2b
Working cross
stitch in two
journeys

French Knot

French knots have been used for details in some of the designs. To work, follow Fig 3, bringing the needle and thread up through the fabric at the exact place where the knot is to be positioned.

Wrap the thread once or twice around the needle (according to the project instructions), holding the thread firmly close to the needle, then twist the needle back through the fabric as close as possible to where it first emerged. Holding the knot down carefully, pull the thread through to the back leaving the knot on the surface, securing it with one small stitch on the back.

Fig 3
Working a
French knot

Long Stitch

This stitch is used in some of the projects. Simply work a long, straight stitch (Fig 4) starting and finishing at the points indicated on the chart.

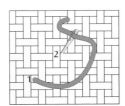

Fig 4
Working a long
stitch

Three-quarter Cross Stitch

Three-quarter cross stitches give more detail to a design and can create the illusion of curves. They are shown by a triangle within a square on the charts. These stitches are easier on evenweave fabric than Aida (see Fig 5). To work on Aida, make a quarter stitch from the corner into the centre of the Aida square, pierce the fabric, and then work a half cross stitch across the other diagonal.

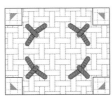

Fig 5
Working
three-quarter
cross stitch

Attaching Beads

Attach seed beads using ordinary sewing thread that matches the fabric colour and a beading needle or very fine 'sharp' needle and a half or whole cross stitch (Fig 6).

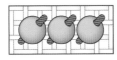

Fig 6
Attaching beads

Making Up

The embroideries from this book are very versatile and have been made up in many ways. Generally, making up is included with projects but some basic techniques are described here and overleaf.

Making Up into a Card

Many of the designs or parts of the larger designs can be stitched and made up into beautiful greetings cards. You will need: a ready-made card mount (aperture to fit embroidery) and craft glue or double-sided tape.

Trim the edges of the embroidery so it is slightly larger than the card aperture. Apply a thin coat of glue or a strip of double-sided tape to the inside of the card opening. (Note: some card mounts already have this tape in place.) Position the embroidery over the aperture, checking that the stitching is central, and then press down firmly. Fold the spare flap over to cover the back of the embroidery. Stick in place with glue or tape and leave to dry before closing.

You can add a personal touch to ready-made card mounts by gluing on ribbons, bows, beads, buttons, stickers or by adding personal doodles in decorative markers. Visit your local stationery or craft store and explore all the possibilities.

Making Up as a Framed Picture

The designs in this book make great framed pictures. You will need: a picture frame (aperture size to fit embroidery); a piece of plywood or heavyweight card slightly smaller than the frame and adhesive tape or a staple gun.

1 Iron your embroidery and trim the edges if necessary, then centre the embroidery on the plywood or thick card. Fold the edges of the embroidery to the back and use adhesive tape or a staple gun to fix in place. Insert the picture into the frame and secure with adhesive tape or staples.

For an expert finish, with a wider choice of mounts and frames, take your work to a professional framer.

Making a Fridge Magnet

A magnet can feature small motifs or witty sayings. For one magnet you will need: two 10cm (4in) squares of felt; lightweight iron-on interfacing and fusible web and 25.4 x 30.5cm (10 x 12in) self-adhesive photo magnet sheet.

1 Cut iron-on interfacing 2.5cm (1in) larger than the embroidery all around. With the wrong side facing, centre the interfacing and fuse to the embroidery. Trim to three rows beyond the design.

2 Cut fusible web to match the felt size and sandwich between the two felt pieces. Press to fuse. Cut fusible web the same size as the prepared embroidery. Centre the embroidery on the felt square with the fusible web sandwiched between and fuse. To finish, cut a 10cm (4in) square of photo magnet and press on to the back of the felt.

Making up a Tote Bag

A stylish tote bag is straightforward to make and could feature other designs from the book. You will need: 0.5m (½yd) each fabric for tote and lining; 0.5m (½yd) fusible fleece; 1.5m (1½yd) of 3.8cm (1½in) wide ribbon for handles; 1m (1yd) decorative trim; lightweight iron-on interfacing and fusible web; five decorative buttons and permanent fabric glue.

1 Cut iron-on interfacing 2.5cm (1in) larger than the embroidery all around. With the wrong side of your work facing, centre the interfacing and fuse to the embroidery. Trim the embroidery six rows beyond the design.

2 Cut two 43 x 48cm (17in x 19in) rectangles from both the tote and lining fabrics. Cut two similar pieces of fusible fleece and fuse to the wrong side of the lining fabric pieces. Cut out a 7.6cm (3in) square at the bottom corners of all the fabric pieces (Fig 7). Place the lining pieces right sides together and stitch a 1.25cm (½in) seam down the sides and across the bottom. Do the same with the tote pieces but leave a gap in the bottom for turning. Match up the bottom and side seams of each stitched piece and stitch across the corners (Fig 8).

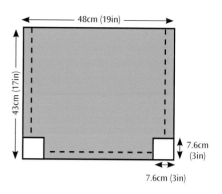

Fig 7 Cut out 7.6cm (3in) squares from the bottom corners

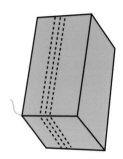

Fig 8 Sewing up the bag

3 With right sides together, place the lining inside the tote, matching the top edge. Cut the ribbon in half and place the pieces between the lining and outside of the tote 15.3cm (6in) apart on the front and back, matching the raw ends with the top edge of the fabric. Stitch a 1.25cm (½in) seam at the top edge. Turn the bag right side out and slipstitch the gap closed. Stitch along the top of the bag 1.25cm (½in) from the finished edge and then again 6mm (¼in) below that.

4 Cut a piece of fusible web the same size as the prepared embroidery, centre the embroidery on the front of the bag with the web behind it and fuse together. Glue the decorative trim along the raw edge of the embroidery starting and ending at centre bottom and attaching a decorative button where the raw ends meet. Attach the remaining buttons to the front and back of the tote at the base of each of the handles.

Making a Mini Sachet

Small designs or parts of larger designs, such as the moth from the Woodland Goddess design, can be used to create pretty sachets. These basic instructions can be adapted as necessary to create larger or smaller sachets.

1 Trim the fabric to within 2.5cm (1in) of the finished embroidery. Cut a second piece of the same fabric the same size. Using one strand of stranded cotton (floss) DMC 434 (or colour to match the embroidery), stitch a running stitch four fabric threads beyond the last row of the embroidery, making the sachet 34 x 34 stitches. Repeat this running stitch around a 34 x 34 stitch area on the blank fabric.

2 Trim both pieces of fabric to within six rows of the running stitch and fold along this line of stitches. Finger press in place, mitring corners. With wrong sides together, use two strands of matching stranded cotton to whip stitch the running backstitches from both pieces, starting at centre bottom. As you go, add a 02038 brilliant copper seed bead to every other stitch. Insert the ends of the twisted cord to create a hanger at the upper left corner and a tassel at the lower right corner securing with whipstitching as you go. Before finishing, stuff with polyester filling and pot-pourri. Finish whipstitching until edges are sealed.

Making a Tassel

A tassel makes a nice finishing touch to many projects and is easy to make.

1 Cut a piece of stiff card, about 1.25cm (½in) longer than the desired size of the tassel. Choose a thread colour to match your project and wrap it around the card to the desired thickness (Fig 9).

2 Slip a length of thread through the top of the tassel and tie in a knot. Slide the threads off the card. Bind the top third of the tassel with length of thread and then trim the tassel ends.

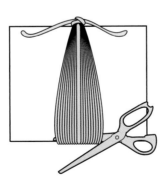

Fig 9 Making a tassel

Making a Twisted Cord

A twisted cord is perfect for embellishing projects, for creating decorative edgings and making hanging cords. The mini sachet below has a twisted cord made from various thread colours.

1 Choose a colour or group of colours in stranded cottons (or other threads) to match your embroidery. Cut a minimum of four lengths at least four times the finished length required and fold in half. Ask a friend to hold the two ends while you slip a pencil through the loop at the other end. Twist the pencil and continue twisting until kinks appear (Fig 10). Walk slowly towards your partner and the cord will twist.

2 Smooth out the kinks from the looped end and secure with a knot at the other end. The cord is now ready to use and can be slipstitched around the edge of a project, or used as a hanger.

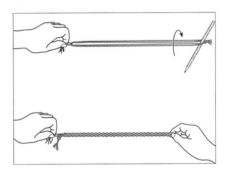

Fig 10 Making a twisted cord

Stitching Tips

✦ The fabric you are stitching on should be at least 5cm (2in) larger all round than the finished size of the stitching, to allow for making up.

✦ When you have cut the length of stranded cotton you need, usually about 46cm (18in), separate all the strands and then thread your needle with the number of strands needed.

✦ For neat stitching, work the top diagonal on cross stitches so they all face the same direction.

✦ Work the backstitches after the cross stitches to avoid the solid line of the backstitch being broken.

✦ If using an embroidery hoop, avoid placing it over worked stitches.

About the Author

Joan Elliott has been creating needlework designs for over 30 years, enchanting stitching enthusiasts the world over with her unique humour and charm. Design Works Crafts Inc in the United States (see Suppliers) produce kits of many of her designs and she remains their leading artist. Her debut book for David & Charles, *A Cross Stitcher's Oriental Odyssey*, was followed by the equally successful *Cross Stitch Teddies*. Other books followed – *Cross Stitch Sentiments & Sayings, Native American Cross Stitch* and *Cross Stitch Wit & Wisdom* – allowing her to combine her creativity as an artist with her love of language, to create projects that amuse, motivate and inspire all stitchers. Joan divides her time between Brooklyn, New York and southern Vermont, and feels blessed that she and her husband have the opportunity to enjoy and share the many joys and experiences that both city and country life have to offer.

Suppliers

Charles Craft Inc
PO Box 1049, Laurinburg,
NC 28353, USA
tel: 910 844 3521
email: ccraft@carolina.net
www.charlescraft.com
For fabrics for cross stitch including Fiddler's Light Aida and Monaco evenweave and many useful pre-finished items (Coats Crafts UK supply some Charles Craft products in the UK)

Coats Crafts UK
PO Box 22, Lingfield Estate,
McMullen Road, Darlington, County
Durham DL1 1YQ, UK
tel: 01325 365457
(for a list of stockists)
For Anchor stranded cotton (floss) and other embroidery supplies. Coats also supplies some Charles Craft products

Design Works Crafts Inc.
170 Wilbur Place, Bohemia,
New York 11716, USA
tel: 631 244 5749
fax: 631 244 6138
email: customerservice@
designworkscrafts.com
For cross stitch kits featuring designs by Joan Elliott

DMC Creative World
Pullman Road, Wigston,
Leicestershire LE18 2DY, UK
tel: 0116 281 1040
fax: 0116 281 3592
www.dmc/cw.com
For stranded cotton (floss) and other embroidery supplies

Joan Elliott
www.joanelliottdesign.com

Framecraft Miniatures Ltd
Unit 3, Isis House, Linden Road,
Brownhills, Walsall, West Midlands,
WS8 7BW, UK
tel: 01543 373 076
fax: 01543 453 154
www.framecraft.com
USA Distributor:
Anne Brinkley Designs, Inc
3895B N Oracle Rd, Tuscon,
AZ 85705, USA
tel: 520 888 1462
fax: 520 888 1483
For wooden trinket bowls and boxes, notebook covers, pincushions, key rings and other pre-finished items with cross stitch inserts, including trinket bowl code W4E

Impress Cards & Craft Materials
1 James Watt Close, Gapton Hall
Industrial Estate, Great Yarmouth,
Norfolk, NR31 0NX, UK
tel: 01986 781422
fax: 01986 781677
email: sales@impresscards.co.uk
www.impresscards.com
For card mounts and cross stitch finishing accessories

Kreinik Manufacturing Company, Inc
1708 Gihon Rd, Parkersburg,
WV 26102, USA
tel: 1-800-537-2166
fax: (304) 428-4326
email: information@kreinik.com
www.kreinik.com
For a wide range of metallic threads, blending filaments and metallic cords

Madeira Threads (UK) Ltd
PO Box 6, Thirsk, North Yorkshire
YO7 3YX, UK
tel: 01845 524880
email: info@madeira.co.uk
www.madeira.co.uk
For Madeira stranded cotton (floss) and other embroidery supplies

Market Square (Warminster) Ltd
Wing Farm, Longbridge Deverill,
Warminster, Wiltshire BA12 7DD, UK
tel: 01985 841041
fax: 01985 541042
For work boxes and trinket boxes

Polstitches
tel: 01559 370406
email: polstitches@tiscali.co.uk
www.polstitchesdesigns.co.uk
For hand-dyed cross stitch fabrics and threads

Sudberry House
12 Colton Road, East Lyme,
CT 06333 USA
tel: 860 739 6951
email: sales@sudberry.com
www.sudberry.com
For quality wooden products for displaying needlework, including the wooden box (page 87) code 99531

Wichelt Imports (Mill Hill)
N162 Hwy 35, Stoddard,
WI 54658, USA
tel: 800 356 9516
fax: 608 788 6040
www.wichelt.com
For Mill Hill beads, Jobelan evenweave and other cross stitch fabrics, wooden bell pulls, buttons and accessories

Zweigart/Joan Toggit Ltd
262 Old Brunswick Road, Suite E,
Piscataway, NJ 08854-3756 USA
tel: 732 562 8888
email: info@zweigart.com
www.zweigart.com
For a large selection of cross stitch fabrics including Cashel Linen® and Jubilee®

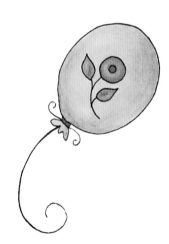

Acknowledgments

Once again, my heartfelt thanks to each of the creative women and gentleman that put their talented hands to work stitching the models for this book: Bev Ritter, Rindy Richards, Judi Trochimiak, Lisa Rabon, Lynda Moss, MaryAnn Stephens, Lori West, Debbie Fitzgerald, Lois Schultz, Sharon Shutjer, and Charlie Rosenberger. I continue to be amazed each time I first see my designs come alive through your work.

   With this, my sixth book for David & Charles, my admiration and fondness for the entire team at David & Charles grows even stronger. To Bethany Dymond for her organizing skills, to Charly Bailey for her beautiful layouts and to Kim Sayer and Karl Adamson for their lovely photography, my sincerest thanks. To my commissioning editor Cheryl Brown who has been supportive and enthusiastic every step of the way and, as always, has played a tremendous role in making this book the best it can be – thank you. Finally, to Lin Clements, my editor, I once again want to send my deepest appreciation for your talents and friendship.

Index

ageing gracefully 56–65
    photo case 60, 65
    pictures 56–9, 62–3

backstitch 101, 103
bags 34–5, 38, 102
beads, attaching 101
birthday picture 58–9, 63
book covers
    fix-it-chick notebook 44, 49
    recipe 42–3, 50–1
    sisters album 86–7, 90
    tiara notebook 11, 15
bovines, indulgent 74–81
box
    keepsake 87, 91
    trinket 68, 70
butterfly sachet 19

cards
    carp 95
    making up 101
    mushroom 19
    violet 68, 72
charts, using 100
chequebook cover 10, 15
chores 36, 40–55
coasters, gossip 26, 29, 31
coffee time 24, 26, 30–1
cooking
    pincushion 49
    recipe book 41–3, 50–1
    trivet 43, 49
cord, making 103
cosmetics case 61, 64
cross stitch 101
cushion, stitching angel 46–7, 54–5

daughter, keepsake box 87, 91
design size 100, 103
diet bovines 74–81
do-it-yourself
    notebook 44, 49
    picture 44–5, 52–3
    pincushion 49
domestic angels 40–55

fabric 100, 103, 104
finishing work 100, 103
flowers
    language of 66, 67
    picture 67–8, 70–3
    primrose trinket pot 68
    rose pillow 69
    violet card 68
frames 100
French knot 101
fridge magnets 76–7, 102
friends 26–9, 31

goddess
    sea 92–9
    woodland 16–23
grandmother, picture 85, 89

hoops 103

key ring, stiletto 8, 15

long stitch 101

materials 100, 104
mothers, hanging 83–4, 88
mushroom cards 19

needles 100

photographs
    sisters album 86–7, 90
    young at heart case 60, 65
pictures
    ageing gracefully 56–9, 62–3
    beverage friends 25–31
    do-it-yourself 44–5, 52–3
    grandmother 85, 89
    making up 102
    sea goddess 93–4, 96–9
    shopping 7, 8–9, 12–14
    sweet life 74, 76, 78–81
    Victorian garden 67–8, 70–1
    woodland goddess 16–18, 20–3
    working women 32–9
pillow, rose 69, 70
pincushions, domestic angels 48–9
pressing 100
primrose trinket pot 68, 70

rabbits 17, 23
rose pillow 69, 70

sachets
    butterfly 19
    making up 103
    seahorse 95
sea goddess 92–9
seahorse sachet 95
sewing angels
    cushion 46–7, 54–5
    pincushion 48
shopping
    bag 34–5, 38, 102

chequebook cover 10, 15
    pictures 7, 8–9, 12–14
sisters, album 86–7, 90
starting work 100, 103
stiletto key ring 8, 15
stitches 101, 103
suppliers 104
sweet indulgence 74–81

tassel, making 103
tea time 24, 26, 28–9
techniques 100
thread 100, 103, 104
three-quarter cross stitch 101
tiara notebook 11, 15
trinket pot 68, 70
trivet, cook's 43, 49

violet card 68, 72

wall hanging, mothers 83–4, 88
washing 100
woodland goddess 16–23
working women 32–9